Your Towns and Cities in the Gr

Weymouth, Dorchester and Portland

in the Great War

This book is dedicated to my late mother-in-law, Penelope Dunn (née Sandes), a lifelong diarist and custodian of her family's diaries, without whom this book would never have been written.

Your Towns and Cities in the Great War

Weymouth, Dorchester and Portland

in the Great War

Jacqueline Wadsworth

Pen & Sword
MILITARY

First published in Great Britain in 2015 by
PEN & SWORD MILITARY
an imprint of
Pen and Sword Books Ltd
47 Church Street
Barnsley
South Yorkshire S70 2AS

Copyright © Jacqueline Wadsworth 2015

ISBN 978 1 47382 272 6

Printed and bound in England
by CPI Group (UK) Ltd, Croydon, CR0 4YY

Typeset in Times New Roman

Pen & Sword Books Ltd incorporates the imprints of
Pen & Sword Archaeology, Atlas, Aviation, Battleground, Discovery,
Family History, History, Maritime, Military, Naval, Politics, Railways,
Select, Social History, Transport, True Crime, and Claymore Press,
Frontline Books, Leo Cooper, Praetorian Press, Remember When,
Seaforth Publishing and Wharncliffe.
For a complete list of Pen and Sword titles please contact
Pen and Sword Books Limited
47 Church Street, Barnsley, South Yorkshire, S70 2AS, England
E-mail: enquiries@pen-and-sword.co.uk
Website: **www.pen-and-sword.co.uk**

Contents

Introduction and Acknowledgements

THE AIM OF this book is to give a flavour of what life was like during the Great War in Weymouth, Dorchester and Portland. To this end I have gathered together memories of those who were there, diaries and letters that were written at the time, and contemporary photographs, newspaper reports and various other documents which I hope furnish a colourful account of those bleak days.

A number of people and organisations provided invaluable support during my research, and I would like to extend my sincere thanks to the following: Jim Barker, Duncan Barrett, John Broom, Geoffrey Carter, Dr Colin Chapman, Michael Day, Dorset History Centre, Dorset Library Service, the Dunn family, Anne McCosker, Shirley Mitchell and the ladies at Portland Heritage Trust, Tina Morley and Barbara Taylor, Eddie Prowse, Richard Samways at Weymouth Museum, the Sandes family, Eric Scott, and the keepers of the Smythe family records in Australia.

Thank you also to my husband and daughters, Ralph, Frances and Catherine Dunn, who read through the chapters as they were written and were never less than encouraging.

Last but not least, I would like to thank Jen Newby for her helpful and skilful editing.

Chapter One

1914 – EUROPEAN CONFLICT THREATENS PEACEFUL SHORES

AFTER A WET and miserable start to 1914, the people of South Dorset breathed a sigh of relief when the spring sunshine finally arrived, spreading its warmth over the chalky downs of the Ridgeway and then south towards Weymouth Bay. As communities gradually came back to life after the long winter, they started to make plans for the traditional summer events – fêtes, picnics, carnivals – just as their forefathers always had. Few noticed the clouds of conflict brewing ominously over Europe, nor did they have any way of knowing just how quickly Britain would be drawn into war later that summer. For the moment, they were busy with the affairs of everyday life.

On the Isle of Portland, local children had spent the winter saving their pennies and counting down the days to their annual Sunday school outing. Organized by the Band of Hope, a Temperance organisation for

Strollers enjoy the spring sunshine on Weymouth Parade in this photograph taken before the war. *(Courtesy of Weymouth Library, Ref: L942.331 Wey.12).*

Children pictured early last century at Easton Clock Tower on Portland: the annual Sunday school outing was the only opportunity many had to leave the island.

(Courtesy of Portland Heritage Trust).

working class youth, it was one of the few opportunities many had to venture off Portland. When the big day arrived in May, well over a hundred youngsters crowded on to the platform at Easton Station, where a special train awaited. At the sound of the guard's whistle the engine pulled away, trundling down the island's steep incline, over the water to join the main line at Melcombe Regis, and onward to the village of Upwey for a day of fun and games, topped off by a fine strawberry tea.

Excitement of an entirely different kind was mounting among the well-to-do young ladies of Weymouth, as they prepared for the visit of a squadron of French warships in June 1914. A ball had been arranged to mark the occasion, which promised to be one of the social events of the year. It was being held at Sidney Hall, which then stood at the bottom of Boot Hill, and one of the 36 hostesses was Margaret Sneyd-Kynnersley, a widow who lived in Greenhill with her four daughters, Kitty, Sylvia, Madge and Rosie.

The French arrived at Portland Harbour on a misty Saturday morning. 'To time precisely, a smudge of smoke on the horizon and merging from its mistiness the funnels of the French cruisers appeared, while a little later the destroyers and submarines also showed up,' wrote a reporter from *The Times*. 'Joy week for Weymouth and the French,' announced Sylvia Sneyd-Kynnersley in her diary. She and her sisters were lifelong diary-writers and – as will be seen in this book – their journals described in colourful detail how the war affected ordinary people's lives.

The Sneyd-Kynnersley sisters were dressed in the finest Edwardian fashions Weymouth's drapery stores could offer when they attended the ball three days later, and the evening proved a great success. 'Danced till daylight, 3.30 ... Ripping dance,' wrote Madge.

In July it was the turn of Dorchester's army wives to enjoy a day in the sun. Their husbands of the 3rd (Special Reserve) Battalion, the Dorsetshire Regiment, were away attending the annual summer training camp at Preston, on the eastern edge of Weymouth, and their families had been invited to visit. 'The men ... are now in the third week of their month's training at Preston, and all of them are quite tanned by their exposure to the sun during their evolutions [exercises] and amusement in the open air,' reported the *Southern Times*. 'They have had fairly good weather up to the present and have borne the discomforts of a few wet days with cheerfulness.'

Special attention had been paid to 'the aggressive side of modern warfare',

'Joy week for Weymouth,' wrote Sylvia Sneyd-Kynnersley in her diary.
(Courtesy of the Sandes family).

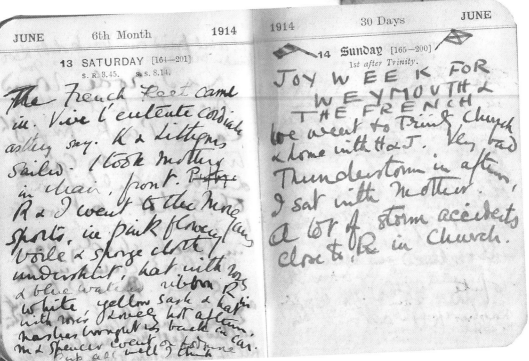

Edwardian ladies take the air on Chesil Beach, but war would soon be approaching these shores. *(Courtesy of the Sandes family).*

continued the report. One morning a sham attack was made on an old coastguard station close to the camping ground, which was quickly captured at the expense of very little ammunition. 'In the afternoon the wives and children of the sergeants came out from Dorchester and were entertained at the camp, spending a very pleasant time.'

When the camp was wound up on Saturday, 1 August, tension was mounting on the Continent after the assassination of Archduke Franz Ferdinand, heir to the Austro-Hungarian Empire, in Sarajevo. Alliances between the major European countries were activated, armies were mobilised and Germany invaded neutral Belgium. Britain demanded Germany's immediate withdrawal from its ally's territory, which was refused and, as a result, war was declared. The lives of ordinary people not only in Britain but across the world were about to be turned upside down.

With the balmy days of summer camp still fresh in their minds, the soldiers of Dorset's 3rd Battalion would soon come face to face with the realities of 'modern warfare'. Meanwhile, the Sneyd-Kynnersley sisters found themselves back at Sidney Hall – this time in the uniform of Red Cross nurses – when it was turned into a military hospital. And Portland's children would now donate their hard-earned pennies to buy comforts for the men at the Front, perhaps their own fathers, uncles and brothers. Conflict was lapping at the peaceful shores of South Dorset.

Britain's declaration of war against Germany was issued at 11.00pm on 4 August. At first there was great excitement throughout the county. Members of Dorset Council could hardly contain their exuberance when the chairman, Lord Portman, proposed a motion of support for the war. Every sentence he spoke was roundly cheered, according to a report in the *Western Gazette*:

'They [the Government] were bound to go to war – (hear, hear) – for they could not have deserted France in her trouble. (Hear, hear.) If they had deserted France at this crisis they could never have held their heads up again – (applause) – either in Europe of the Empire. (Renewed applause.)'

It wasn't long, however, before excitement was tempered by unease. The country had been at peace with her European neighbours for a century and therefore no-one knew quite what to expect. Many householders began laying in emergency stocks, which promptly led to price rises: 'Food going up so Sylvia & I went to town and bought 21lbs biscuits, 1 ton coal, 12lbs jam, 4lbs tea, also cocoa, beans, macaroni, Horlick, flour and soap, candles!' remarked Madge Sneyd-Kynnersley in early August.

Notices appeared in newspapers warning the public not to panic-buy, like this one from the *Southern Times*:

'The Weymouth Master Bakers' Association appeal to all their Customers to assist in this great National Crisis by TAKING ONLY THE USUAL QUANTITIES of BREAD and FLOUR and Paying for the same as soon as possible. All bakers have now to PAY CASH for some of the Materials they use. It is therefore impossible to give more than a WEEK'S CREDIT to anyone at the present time.'

A warning from the Weymouth Master Bakers' Association printed in the *Southern Times* during August 1914.

Weymouth
Master Bakers' Association

Appeal to all their Customers to assist them in this great National Crisis by TAKING ONLY the USUAL QUANTITIES of BREAD and FLOUR and Paying for the same as soon as possible.

All Bakers have now to PAY CASH for some of the Materials they use. It is, therefore, impossible to GIVE MORE than a WEEK'S CREDIT to anyone at the present time.

HELP ONE ANOTHER !

DO NOT BOYCOTT !

SUPPORT YOUR REGULAR BAKER !

HOUSE AND ESTATE AGENTS.   FIXTURES.

(Above, opposite and overleaf) Snapshots taken on Weymouth seafront show troops (thought to be Canadian) mustering one cold winter's day. At the outbreak of war, townspeople were unused to such military scenes. *(Courtesy of the Sandes family).*

Some traders, like the local motor and cycle company Tilley's, made it clear that their services had not been disrupted. 'Business as usual,' its advertisement insisted. 'If you have any difficulty with your transport we can help you. Our prices have not been raised.'

Others turned the situation to their advantage. The Maypole Dairy gleefully advertised the fact that its margarine had been made using nuts confiscated from captured German ships. In contrast, V. H. Bennett, which sold a range of goods and could probably claim to be Weymouth's earliest department store, anticipated the need for medical supplies and let it be known that the store was 'fully stocked with all goods necessary for Red Cross meetings'. Their shelves were piled with nurses' aprons, caps, sleeves and dresses, and a free pattern was on offer to any customers buying material to make soldiers' shirts.

The Dorchester furniture store Hannah and Holland put together 'bed sets' for the Red Cross, which comprised: a 3ft iron bedstead with wire-

sprung mattress, soft mattress, bolster, pillow, two blankets, two white sheets and a pillow slip. 'Send your order and cheque for two guineas and we will do the rest,' they assured potential customers.

Army mobilisation was immediate and became particularly evident in the garrison town of Dorchester, home to the Dorsetshire County Regiment. Its thoroughfares were soon bursting with reservists and men from the part-time Territorial Force and Yeomanry, all gathering there to receive orders. This is how the *Dorset County Chronicle* described the scene on 6 August:

> 'The streets of Dorchester to-day have been suggestive of those of a 'leaguered town, in the crowd, the bustle, the excitement, and the many and varied uniforms seen in the throng "hurrying to and fro"... Reservists of the Dorsetshire Regiment are flocking to the Barracks in steady numbers and are being clothed, equipped and armed, after which they are being despatched in convenient batches to join the 1st Battalion at Belfast.'

Bringing the Dorsets' 1st Battalion up to war strength was given priority, so that its troops could proceed quickly from their base in Ireland to

France with the British Expeditionary Force. Consequently, many Dorchester reservists were swiftly despatched to the Emerald Isle. 'The GWR Station was a scene of animation between twelve o'clock and one. Reservists bound for Belfast left amid loud cheers,' reported the *Dorset County Chronicle*. Ten days later, on 16 August, the 1st Battalion had landed at Le Havre.

Such military scenes were far less familiar to the people of Weymouth, who were more accustomed to rubbing shoulders with sailors from Portland Naval Base, one of the Royal Navy's biggest bases. It was, therefore, an eerie sight for Sylvia Sneyd-Kynnersley when hundreds of Royal Welch Fusiliers marched past her home at Greenhill Terrace, as dawn broke one morning. She described the scene thus: 'Woken up last night by soldiers pouring in from Wool at quarter to five. Looked up and saw me at window and laughed and waved! Very sinister it seemed to see them in the dim light.' The men had been recalled to their barracks at the Verne Citadel on Portland and were marching in from Wool Station.

For the first time ever, huge numbers of civilians were now being urged to join the army and fight alongside Britain's professional soldiers. In the past, Britain had relied upon its small but highly-trained Regular Army to take care of conflicts (along with the Royal Navy). But Lord Kitchener, the new Secretary of State for War, believed this force of around 400,000 men would be nowhere near big enough. Unlike most of his contemporaries, he believed that the fighting could last for many years and would demand far more troops than the existing army could supply. Consequently, Kitchener set his sights on raising an additional 500,000 men and, once the Government had given their approval, he appealed directly to the public through newspaper advertisements and posters urging potential volunteers to join up.

Men responded by queueing outside recruitment halls, where they were examined to ensure they were in good health, of suitable height (over 5ft 3in), age (18 to enlist, 19 to serve abroad), possessed sufficiently strong teeth to subsist on the tough army-ration biscuits, and had good enough vision to be able to sight a rifle. Some would then be posted to existing battalions, while others joined entirely new 'service' battalions formed to accommodate Kitchener's volunteer army.

SOUTHERN TIMES, SEPT. 5TH, 1914.

4th BATT. DORSET REGT.

Men of Dorset !

YOUR KING & COUNTRY NEED YOU

Join Your County Battalion.

In consequence of 600 Non-Commissioned Officers and Men of the 4th Dorset (Territorials) having

VOLUNTEERED FOR FOREIGN SERVICE,

500 RECRUITS

Are now needed to complete the Establishment, and

600 RECRUITS

For HOME SERVICE.

OFFICER COMMANDING.

An appeal goes out for the 'Men of Dorset' to enlist in the *Southern Times*, September 1914.

Standards were fairly rigorous in 1914 and by no means all volunteers were accepted, but as the war went on and fewer men came forward requirements were relaxed, and older, less robust recruits would be waved through.

Men's reasons for joining up were varied and often depended on personal circumstances. For the poorest, including many agricultural labourers, the army might have offered the first decent, regular wage they had ever been paid, along with an escape from often miserable living conditions. Slums still existed across the country and the humiliating threat of the workhouse continued to hang over the most desperate. At Fordington, on the east of Dorchester, the insanitary and overcrowded hovels of Mill Street were notorious. Indeed, Thomas Hardy, a Dorchester man himself, had used them as a model for the grim Mixen Lane in his 1886 novel *The Mayor of Casterbridge*. 'It was the hiding place of those who were in distress, and in debt, and trouble of every kind,' he wrote. 'Much that was sad, much that was low, some things that were baneful, could be seen in Mixen Lane.'

Others who were more fortunate still saw their lives stretching before them in the same way their fathers' had: long, physically exhausting shifts at work, a house full of children and only the pub to look forward to in the evening. A large proportion of local men worked at big employers like Lott and Walne's foundry in Fordington, the Devenish Brewery in Weymouth, and Eldridge Pope Brewery in Dorchester. But while these firms provided employees with security, the war offered something that appeared far more attractive to some – adventure abroad.

Duty and patriotism also played an important part in persuading some men to enlist, as did the influence that wives, mothers and sweethearts were encouraged to exert for the good of the country. One War Office poster posed these questions to the women of Britain:

'Do you realise that the safety of your home and children depends on our getting more men NOW?'

'Do you realise that the one word "GO" from you may send another man to fight for our King and Country?

'When the war is over and someone asks your husband or your son what he did in the Great War, is he to hang his head because you would not let him go?

'Won't you help and send a man to join the Army to-day?'

Some women needed little persuasion to get involved, and handed out white feathers – a traditional emblem of cowardice – to any man in the street who was not in uniform and looked, to them, as though he was shirking his duty. The White Feather Campaign was initiated in August 1914 by a retired naval vice-admiral, Charles Penrose-Fitzgerald, and supported by prominent feminists of the day. Although it added to the pressure for men to enlist, it also aroused resentment, when feathers were presented to soldiers home on leave and in civilian clothes, for example, or to men who were employed in vital war industries.

In Weymouth, Sylvia Sneyd-Kynnersley was impressed by a friend who boldly informed men in civilian dress that they ought to be in uniform. She decided to take a leaf out of the same book:

A poster produced by the Parliamentary Recruiting Committee in 1915 urges women to play their part in encouraging men to enlist.

(Courtesy of the Library of Congress, Reproduction No LC-USZC4-10915).

A gathering of the Fleet in Portland Harbour, probably taken in 1912; most of the ships pictured here would join the Grand Fleet in 1914.
(Courtesy of the Geoffrey Carter Collection).

'After tea Kitty, Madge and I walked along cliffs right past the Jordan [at Sutton Poyntz] and said loudly "That man ought to be in uniform" when we met loafers. Don't know if this method is much good but what can one do to make them go?'

Kitchener's appeal met with huge success in the early months of war, and on 5 September the *Southern Times* reported rousing scenes at a local recruitment rally:

'Weymouth worked itself up to a fever heat of enthusiasm on Thursday night for the great and memorable and solemn assembly which was gathered at the King's Statue [on the seafront] in one solid mass of people as the twilight was fading into night, and as great shafts of light from the land forts were sweeping across our

silent Bay to back up Major Groves and the other recruiting officers in finding a worthy contribution from Weymouth to swell Lord Kitchener's Army … The crowd numbered several thousand and from every balcony on the boarding houses opposite there were spectators of the stirring scene.'

Even as soldiers packed their kits bags and bade their families farewell, Britain's Grand Fleet had already moved off to its war stations in the North Sea, in secrecy and under cover of darkness. The Fleet had steamed out of Portland Harbour on 28 July, on the order of Winston Churchill, then First Lord of the Admiralty.

It had been gathered at Weymouth Bay following a Royal Review at Portsmouth, a spectacle that had drawn enormous crowds. Vast new ships were being built in response to rivalry with the rapidly expanding German Navy and the public was left in awe. 'No one privileged to witness the sight in Weymouth Bay towards the end of July, 1914, will ever forget the mighty armada,' reported the *Southern Times*. 'Super-Dreadnought battleships and cruisers by the dozen. Light cruisers and destroyers by the score, the most wonderful fighting units that ever sailed the seas.'

The Fleet had been due to disperse after the Review but, with tension growing in Europe, the ships were ordered to remain in harbour, where they were readied for war instead. Busy scenes ensued, as small boats ferried personal belongings, wardroom furniture and other potentially flammable items from the vessels to dockyard stores. Ammunition was taken on board, including projectiles from the Whitehead Torpedo Works at Wyke Regis, and coaling was underway.

On 28 July, when Austria declared war on Serbia, it was feared by the British Admiralty that the ships would be vulnerable to German attack if they remained in harbour, and men were ordered to return to their ships immediately. Before the sun rose next day, the Grand Fleet had slipped out of Portland Harbour without lights and in radio silence, and was steaming at speed to its war stations in the North Sea. In 1923 Winston Churchill recalled in stirring words the momentous departure that few had witnessed:

'We may now picture this great fleet with its flotillas of cruisers steaming slowly out of Portland Harbour, squadron by squadron, scores of gigantic castles of steel wending their way across the misty, shining sea, like giants bowed in anxious thought. We may picture them again as darkness fell, 18 miles of warships running at high speed and in absolute darkness, through the narrow Straits, bearing with them into the North Sea the safeguard of considerable affairs.'

***

'Bathed, lovely. Tide high. In evening Kitty and I walked all round by Wyke and all way home – place so full of soldiers and fortifications. Everyone at Rodwell uncertain, road has soldiers billeted … Took knives to be sharpened and put bolts on our doors!' Sylvia Sneyd-Kynnersley's diary entry for 11 August 1914 shows just how quickly the conflict became part of everyday life for British people.

Only a week after war had been declared, some 7,000 territorial soldiers were billeted on civilian homes in Rodwell, while men of the 3rd Dorsets, who had recently been on summer camp in Preston, were posted locally to defend the coast around Portland. Fear of enemy sabotage was extreme – hence the knives and bolts in the Sneyd-Kynnersley household – and on more than one occasion rumours were rife that local water supplies had been poisoned. Soldiers mounted guards at vulnerable installations like railway tunnels, reservoirs and the Wyke torpedo works. Frequently they were sent to check for lights flashing from cliff tops, reported by members of the public who feared that German spies were everywhere.

During the early months of the war, Major C. S. Jarvis was stationed at Wyke with the 3rd Dorsets, and decades later he recalled the 'spy mania' with humour in his memoirs, writing with his tongue firmly in his cheek:

'At least twice a week I had to send out patrols to try and locate mysterious lights, obviously signals to enemy ships and submarines, which appeared on Ridgeway Hill, and my all-too-enthusiastic recruits on these wild-goose chases on one occasion opened fire on the car of the GOC [general officer commanding] himself, and on another nearly killed a shepherd who with a lantern was going round his lambing ewes by night. Needless to say neither … would accept any excuse, or see anything funny in the situation.'

These patrols, revealed the Major, were instigated by 'every ancient retired officer' too old for service 'who suspected of activities to help the enemy quite half of his fellow members of the county club, most of the tradesmen in the town, and many of the farmers and agricultural labourers.' Even worse were the 'on-the-shelf old spinsters normally addicted to good works'.

So frequent were the cries of 'spy' that it was hard for Jarvis to take them all seriously and in consequence he appears to have allowed one of the war's most notorious spies to slip through the net. The incident occurred in September 1914 when, according to Jarvis's memoirs, the company quartermaster sergeant (CQMS) at Wyke arrested a man who had been peering into the wire-enclosed army camp. When questioned, he claimed to be an American citizen from the *Tennessee*, a US cruiser which had just docked in Weymouth, after transporting American citizens back from the Continent. He said that, while awaiting an escort out of the town, he had simply come ashore to see the monument to Vice-Admiral Hardy on the high ground above Portesham. On his way

A sketch of Carl Lody, the German spy who gave Major Jarvis the slip, from a photograph taken before his execution in November 1914.

(Illustration by Olivia Haigh).

back he had looked into the camp at Wyke to watch the soldiers at work.

None of this aroused Jarvis's suspicion. He inspected the American's papers and judged them to be in order, shared a whisky and soda with him, accepted a cigar, and an hour later they parted 'on the best of terms'.

The truth was revealed a month or so later, when the CQMS came running up to Jarvis waving a newspaper. In it was a photograph showing the very same 'American', who had just been executed as a spy. 'He's Carl Lody, the German naval officer, and our people were after him and watching his movements, but he gave them the slip,' explained the excited sergeant. 'That was whilst he was down here looking at our Portland defences. Later they caught him in Edinburgh, and yesterday he was shot.'

Lody was executed by firing squad at the Tower of London on 6 November 1914, having posed as an American tourist whilst gathering intelligence about British shipping. He was the first German spy to be executed in Britain during the war.

'Well,' exclaimed Jarvis in his memoir, 'there did not seem to be anything more to be said about it! We had had the most active and dangerous German spy in our hands and had let him go again, but to own up to it now would not help matters. Over the CQMS I felt guilty, and I salved my conscience in his case by strongly recommending him for a commission which he obtained – and there the matter ended.'

Jarvis was not easily rattled, but among the general public fear and suspicion spread rapidly. A breathless Sylvia Sneyd-Kynnersley wrote on 17 October:

'At 5 I heard the Recall bugled outside and went town – knots of people everywhere and great excitement – they say a German submarine is off Portland! and 3 of our big ships sunk (this is untrue

I heard later) Sailors dashing along on bicycles and officers in cars – ship went out. Heard P. Louis of Battenberg is shot as traitor.'

In fact, reports that Prince Louis of Battenberg, Britain's First Sea Lord, had been shot also turned out to be false. Battenberg was of German descent, which made him highly unpopular, and he resigned a few days later. At the request of King George V, he changed his name later in the war and relinquished his German titles.

Germans had long lived and worked quite happily in Britain, but antagonism could spring up almost anywhere during wartime. An article entitled 'Portland's Shame', which appeared in a 1993 edition of the *Free Portland News*, recalled that anti-German feeling on the island during the First World War was 'a considerable skeleton in Portland's cupboard that shows how kind and tolerant people could get carried away by war hysteria.' One German resident on the island was reportedly driven to suicide by the persecution he faced, another was accused of poisoning the water supply at Upwey, and a third was forced to escape a mob by climbing down a drainpipe at the back of his property. The latter is thought to have been Heinrich Schutte, and for him it was only the beginning of a terrible ordeal.

The day after war was declared, the Aliens Restriction Act was hurried through Parliament requiring all German nationals, and other 'enemy aliens', to register with the police so that they could, if necessary, be deported. Heinrich Schutte was arrested at his workplace, the Great Western Railway cargo stage in Weymouth, and charged with 'communicating to another person a sketch, plans, notes, and other documents and information calculated to be useful to the enemy'. He was remanded in custody while the prosecution gathered evidence.

Schutte originally came from Vilsen, in northern Germany, but by 1914 he had been in Britain for more than 20 years. He worked as a shipping clerk and lived with his English wife, Julia, and their two sons and daughter at Castletown on Portland, overlooking the docks, where Julia ran a boarding house. Anti-German feeling may have already forced the family to leave Portland, because when he was arrested Schutte gave his address as Emmadale Road, in the Westham area of Weymouth.

When he appeared again before the magistrates, Schutte's sons, Jack and Willie, and other friends were there to support him. The *Western Times* reporter sketched this thumbnail portrait of Schutte: 'He is over 50 years of age, is heavily built, and has a florid complexion. It is stated that he is a linguist and has knowledge of several languages. His English is spoken with a guttural accent.'

Heinrich Schutte's 'mugshot' appeared in Dorchester Prison's album of prisoners in 1914, as he awaited deportation as an 'enemy alien'.
(Courtesy of Dorset History Centre, Ref: NG/PR/1/D/5/2).

Court proceedings were brief and initially there was cause for celebration when the case was withdrawn, apparently due to lack of evidence. But there was a sting in the tail: Schutte was to be immediately re-arrested under the Aliens Restrictions Act and sent to Dorchester Gaol to await deportation. His solicitor reportedly commented that 'it seemed rather hard on his client that he should be dealt with in this way without any evidence being offered against him.'

A tired-looking Schutte was later photographed at Dorchester Prison and his 'mugshot' took its place in the prison album of local criminals and ne'er-do-wells.

Schutte was duly deported to Germany, where he found work as a watchman. He died there in 1927, leaving a small amount of money to his wife Julia, who died in Dorset. It is not known if Heinrich was ever reunited with his family. His absence is certainly noticeable in a post-war family photograph showing Julia, their son Jack and his wife, and grandson Harold. However, this sad story is complicated by suggestions in Nigel West's book, *Historical Dictionary of World War I Intelligence*, that before the war Schutte had been accused by MI5 of sending details about the movement of Royal Naval vessels, and sketches of Portland defences to Germany. Schutte insisted he had only passed on innocuous information which was openly available.

Too much time has passed for the matter to be unequivocally settled, but Schutte's great-grandson Eric Scott (whose father, Harold, changed the family name to Scott) believes that his great-grandfather was innocent. 'I don't think Heinrich was a spy,' Eric explained in 2014, 'but he was concerned with shipping, and Portland was a naval base in those times, so he could have had sensitive information. One cannot imagine the hatred that arose at the start of the war. Though probably understandable for that time, it was extremely sad for the family.'

Both of Heinrich Schutte's sons served in the British Army during the Great War; one fought in France and the other was a master tailor with the Middlesex Regiment.

War now took priority over most aspects of life in South Dorset. As a result there was little families could do to prevent the horses they had always depended

The family Heinrich Schutte left behind: his wife, Julia, is pictured with their son, Jack, his wife, Jane, and grandson Harold.
(Courtesy of Eric Scott).

upon for their livelihoods being requisitioned for the Front. The army needed animals to pull artillery, wagons and ambulances, to carry supplies and munitions, and for the cavalry. Although the owners were compensated, it didn't stop their losses being keenly felt. During the early days of the war, the *Dorset County Chronicle* reported:

'Another sharp reminder of the unpleasant exigencies of war was given to the agricultural population of the district today, when at many farms horses were seized unceremoniously by the requisition of the military authorities, without regard to needs of harvesting, and some were even removed from carriers' carts in the streets of Dorchester.'

It wasn't just farmers and tradesmen who had to give up their animals,

A horse is taken in hand at a First World War British Army camp in South Dorset: many animals were requisitioned locally, causing hardship for their owners. *(Courtesy of the Dunn family).*

as the article showed: 'No respect of persons was shown by the authorities in making good the equine shortage and the pick of the stables of many gentlemen in the neighbourhood had to be yielded to urgent military necessity.'

However, as the local population of horses diminished, Tilley's, the local motor engineers, spotted a business opportunity and placed this advert in the *Southern Times* on 15 August: 'Are you inconvenienced by the shortage of horses; if so why not try a Ford delivery van? Price from £130, absolutely reliable, exceptionally low running cost.'

On Portland, one of the local children who had enjoyed the Sunday school trip to Upwey back in May had already seen some profound changes to his young life: 'From that year [1914], nothing was ever the same,' recalled William Swailes many years later. His father, a retired Royal Navy dispenser, was called up as a reservist and worked

Motor engineers Tilley's stepped in when horses were in short supply with this advert, which appeared in the *Southern Times* on 15 August, 1914.

Are you inconvenienced by the SHORTAGE of HORSES; if so, why not try a **FORD DELIVERY VAN,** price from **£130,** absolutely reliable, exceptionally low running cost.

FULL PARTICULARS AND DEMONSTRATION FROM :

TILLEY'S,

MOTOR ENGINEERS,

WEYMOUTH and DORCHESTER.

long shifts on the island. Although it is not clear exactly what William's father did, his working patterns meant that his children had to take meals over to him from their home in Augusta Road, Tophill. William takes up the story:

> 'My father was called up as a first reservist during the war … He was 24 hours on and 12 off. That meant that we children had to take his meals down to him which we did throughout the winter with a three mile walk there and back. As the war escalated there were sentries by the 9.2 guns on East Weare [a battery overlooking Weymouth Bay] and out of the darkness we would be challenged. "Halt! Who goes there?" This coming out of the night used to scare us. In the end my sisters weren't allowed to go, it was only me, a boy of about nine.'

On these solitary walks, William found ways to entertain himself as he approached the sentry:

> 'I'd got to know the whole of the challenge by then, it should have been "Halt, who goes there, friend of foe?" One night, coming up I thought to myself … I'll wait until he gives the "correct" call as I thought. When I got in line with him (he was behind great tall railings and barbed wire fencing) a challenge rang out "Halt Who goes there?" Well, I thought to myself, I'll wait till he says "Friend or foe?" I waited on and then I heard the sound of the breech block of his gun go, and I sang out "Friend!" – I didn't wait for the bullet to be fired!'

It was a sensible decision. Although William may not have read it, the following notice (which included plenty of capital letters for additional emphasis) had been issued by Brigadier General A. C. Currie, Commander, Portland Fortress, and published in the local paper:

> 'ALL PERSONS are WARNED that if they approach positions guarded by Sentries they must immediately and implicitly OBEY the orders of the SENTRY. Should the Sentry order "Hands up", both hands must be raised above the head and kept up until permission is given to lower them. The SENTRIES HAVE INSTRUCTIONS TO SHOOT if their ORDERS are not INSTANTLY OBEYED.'

Portland Harbour bristled with defences against the very real threat posed by German U-boats and torpedoes. In November 1914, Madge Sneyd-Kynnersley noted in her diary: 'German submarine in bay last night, big gun fired at 4.30. It was sunk.'

The only measure taken to protect the harbour in the early months was the addition of nets to block the entrances. These worked well on the north and east sides, but not at the southern entrance where they could be pulled out of position by strong tides. Here, more robust measures were needed and on 4 November 1914 an obsolete battleship, the HMS *Hood*, was scuttled and sunk to block the gap in the breakwater. She came to rest upside down and today her hull and crushed superstructure form a popular site for divers.

***

As the end of the year approached, hopes that the conflict would be over by Christmas, as many had forecast, were beginning to fade. Across the Channel in France and Belgium, the British Expeditionary Force, which included men of the 1st Dorsets, had been engaged in fierce fighting since August. Both sides had suffered heavy casualties, with neither gaining the upper hand, and as 1914 drew to a close exhausted soldiers began digging in for the winter. This was the beginning of trench warfare on the Western Front.

On the other side of the world, the 2nd Battalion, the Dorsetshire Regiment, had sailed from its pre-war base in India to Mesopotamia, where Turkey – soon to become an ally of Germany – was posing a threat to British oil supplies. The 2nd Dorsets landed in the Persian Gulf that November, marking the beginning of an unhappy episode which would lead to the infamous 'siege of Kut-al-Amara' (a story to be told in Chapter Three).

The Great War's early battles were fought by the highly-trained, professional soldiers of Britain's Regular Army, but as casualties mounted they would gradually be replaced by the far less experienced volunteers of Kitchener's Army. At the end of 1914, these new recruits were still being trained at home and they did not start arriving at the Front in large numbers until 1916, in readiness for the Battle of the Somme, from which many would never return. Tragically, some didn't even make it that far.

Frank Adams, a dairyman from Fordington, Dorchester, was only 15 when he enlisted in August 1914. Standing just 5ft 2in tall and weighing 7st 12lb, he must have aroused the recruiting officer's suspicions, but Adams claimed to be 19 and that is what the officer chose to believe. Frank was duly posted to the 3rd Battalion, the Dorsetshire Regiment which was stationed on the Home Front to defend the local area and train troops. Frank was sent to Upton Camp at Ringstead, to guard Weymouth waterworks. He had just celebrated his sixteenth birthday when he was accidentally shot and killed, while larking around at the barracks one evening with a good friend, who had been unaware that the rifle he held was loaded. Frank's coffin was borne on a gun carriage to Weymouth Cemetery, where he was buried. His gravestone still stands today, one of many beautifully preserved by the Commonwealth War Graves Commission, but the only one in the cemetery without the soldier's age at death on the inscription.

A terrific storm hit the Dorset coast on 11 December and the Weymouth lifeboat was forced to put out in atrocious conditions to rescue the crew of a French schooner that had been driven up on to the beach at Greenhill. Thankfully, all were taken off alive. Five days later, however, news of a far more ominous nature came through from the east coast of England: the towns of Whitby, Scarborough and Hartlepool had been bombarded by German ships; 137 civilians were killed and 592 wounded. Britain was outraged. 'Considerable loss of life and many buildings shattered. Disgraceful breach of conventions as no notice was given,' declared Sylvia Sneyd-Kynnersley. The bombing was recalled later recalled on recruiting posters with the slogan 'Remember Scarborough'.

The omens for a happy Christmas may not have been good, but the people of South Dorset did their best to get into the festive spirit despite the conflict. There was excitement in Weymouth about the Pavilion Theatre's 'grand spectacular pantomime' *Jack and the Beanstalk*, which began on Boxing Day. And in Dorchester children pestered their parents to take them to Wood's Domestic Stores, where 'a grand assortment of toys from 1d upwards' was on sale. According to the *Weymouth Telegram*, shops were as busy as ever for one simple reason, war work had put

No age was given on Private Frank Adams' gravestone at Weymouth Cemetery. This young recruit was only 16 when he was accidentally killed – two years short of the enlistment age.

(Photograph by the author).

extra money into the pockets of ordinary people:

> 'Among a certain class there is greater prosperity than ever before. It has been conclusively proved that the majority of wives of servicemen are better off than before, and with mechanics and tradesmen working at high pressure for months past, the close of the present year has not brought to them the distress which many have known formerly.'

Soldiers at the Front sent home beautifully embroidered postcards to wish their loved ones a happy Christmas. Worked by French and Belgian women in their homes, the cards – although expensive – proved extremely popular throughout the war and were treasured by the families of servicemen.

There was a certain amount of festive spirit in the trenches too, which famously manifested itself in what became known as the Christmas Truce. In pockets along the Western Front, soldiers on both sides laid down their arms and met on No Man's Land to chat and exchange gifts. Such scenes were witnessed at St Yves in northern France, where soldiers of the Royal Warwickshire Regiment were posted.

Christmas greetings from the Western Front: one of the thousands of embroidered postcards sent home by soldiers to their families. *(Courtesy of David and Lorraine Judge).*

Among them was Sergeant Major George Beck, of Portland, who wrote in his diary on 24 December:

> 'Germans shout over to us and ask us to play them at football and also not to fire and they would do likewise. At 2am (25th) a German band went along the trenches playing Home Sweet Home and God Save the King which sounded grand and made everyone think of home. During the night several of our fellows went over "No Man's Land" to German lines and was given a drink and cigars.'

These extraordinary scenes continued for the next three days, with soldiers helping to bury each other's dead. On Christmas Day Beck wrote:

Sergeant Major George Beck, of Portland, who served with the Royal Warwickshire Regiment at St Yves, northern France, during the winter of 1914.
(Courtesy of Dorset History Centre, Ref: D.1820/1/2).

'Not one shot was fired. English and German soldiers intermingled and exchanged souvenirs. Germans very eager to exchange almost anything for our "Bully Beef" and jam. Majority of them know French fluently. A few men of the Regiment assisted in burying the dead of the Somerset Light Infantry who were killed on 19.12.14. Fine frosty day. Very cold.'

On 26 December:

'Unofficial truce kept up and our own fellows intermingled still with the Germans. No rifle shots fired, but our artillery fired a few rounds on the German 3rd and 4th lines and Germans retaliated with a few rounds on D Coys [Company's] trenches. Two wounded.'

'Christmas Day. Not one shot was fired.' An extract from Sergeant Major George Beck's diary, recounting the truce of 1914.
(Courtesy of Dorset History Centre, Ref: D.1820/1/7).

And on 27 December: 'No sniping. A few whiz bangs [shells] on D Coys trenches. One wounded.'

Normal fighting was thereafter resumed and would continue relentlessly for the next four years. George Beck survived the war, returning to Portland, where he settled down with his wife and worked as an inspector with the National Omnibus Company. The Christmas Truce fizzled out as the New Year began and, although small pockets of peace were reported during the following Christmas, it would never be repeated in the same way.

Chapter Two

1915 – GERMAN PoWS AND WOUNDED AUSSIES 'INVADE' THE LOCAL AREA

THE LIGHTS ALONG Weymouth seafront went out in January 1915 and the town was plunged into darkness. 'Nice lights are all blacked out now along front for fear of Zeppelins etc. Very dark,' wrote Madge Sneyd-Kynnersley in her diary on 13 January. All over the country

Public anger over German Zeppelin attacks during the First World War is reflected in this sketch (probably by a soldier, see note on the right-hand side) in the autograph book of Maggie Watson, the daughter of a Weymouth publican. *(Courtesy of Tina Morley / The Western Front Association).*

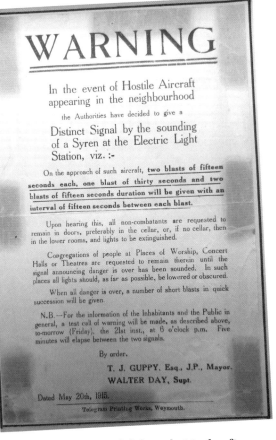

This poster, explaining what to do after an air raid warning, was displayed in Weymouth in 1915.

(Courtesy of Weymouth Museum, Ref: LH/WA/002).

blackouts were being imposed because of the threat of attack by German airships, and the first raid came on the night of 19 January, when bombs were dropped on Great Yarmouth and King's Lynn, killing four civilians and injuring 16.

The British public was outraged that ordinary people had been targeted – it was something for which they were completely unprepared because, for the previous 100 years Britain's conflicts had been fought overseas, often in far corners of the Empire, without threat to home shores. The mood of the country was summed up by a sketch drawn in an autograph book belonging to Maggie Watson, the daughter of a Weymouth publican. 'But mother had done nothing wrong, had she Daddy?' pleads a young girl in the caption, as she tries to comfort her father.

Householders were now ordered to keep their curtains tightly closed at night. Car owners were forbidden to use headlights; side lamps only were permitted. Even trams had to have curtains pulled across their passenger windows. These restrictions were imposed under the new Defence of the Realm Act (universally known as DORA), which allowed the Government to prosecute anyone whose actions were deemed 'to jeopardize the success of the operations of His Majesty's forces or to assist the enemy'. The act came into force in August 1914 and, as the war progressed, new restrictions were added which covered every possible detail of life. Some were predictable, like press censorship; others less so, like the ban on loitering near bridges and tunnels, or whistling for taxis in case the sound was mistaken for an air raid siren.

The main targets of the German airships were industrial areas, army camps and munitions factories, and although Dorset was never hit, the fear was always present. Summonses were issued promptly if chinks of light were spotted in local homes, and the following notice was issued by the mayor of Weymouth, giving details of air raid warnings:

'In the event of hostile aircraft appearing in the neighbourhood, two blasts of fifteen seconds each, one blast of thirty seconds and two blasts of fifteen seconds duration will be given with an interval of fifteen seconds between each blast.'

Disaster had already come dangerously close to home on New Year's Day 1915, when the battleship HMS *Formidable* was torpedoed and sunk in Lyme Bay by a German submarine. The *Formidable* was hit as she returned from a firing exercise under bright moonlight and nearly 600 crewmen drowned or died of hypothermia in the freezing waters. Among those who perished was the Captain, Noel Loxley, who had remained on the bridge with his fox terrier, Bruce, overseeing the evacuation of his ship. Two weeks later, this paragraph appeared in the *Western Gazette*:

'The body of the dog Bruce, the companion of Captain Noel Loxley, of HMS *Formidable*, has been washed ashore at Abbotsbury, near Weymouth. Wreckage from the battleship is being washed up on Chesil Beach. A damaged pinnace has been found on the bank. It contained portions of naval uniforms and two silk handkerchiefs.'

Tucked away in the hills, Dorchester was a safe distance from coastal dangers, but the town would soon have its own dramatic tales to tell, for a huge prisoner of war camp had been established at the former artillery barracks on its western edge and German soldiers were now arriving there in large numbers.

Dorchester Prison Camp was one of the largest in Britain and at its peak accommodated almost 4,500 men – equivalent to around half the pre-war population of Dorchester. It served as the 'parent camp' for the army's Southern Command area. For most of the war captured combatants were held there, but the first to arrive had been Austrian and German civilians who were living in Britain at the outbreak of hostilities. They were now either considered a threat to national security or held to prevent the possibility of their returning home to join up. A photograph taken at the time shows a group of these men being marched through

German prisoners arriving in Dorchester.

Civilian 'alien' prisoners are escorted through the streets of Dorchester during the early weeks of war by soldiers with fixed bayonets.
(Courtesy of Dr Colin Chapman).

Dorchester by soldiers with fixed bayonets – whatever threat the foreigners posed was obviously taken seriously.

The first batch of 18 Germans arrived by train at Dorchester West Station on 10 August 1914. More were to follow, including merchant seamen who had been taken off ships in British waters. Sylvia Sneyd-Kynnersley witnessed one such arrest in Weymouth Bay in September 1914: 'Mother and I walked down after tea and saw the Austrian steamer being brought into the harbour as a prize, searched by soldiers and crew taken to Dorchester – prisoners.'

These civilian internees came from all walks of life and included engineers, professional men, merchants and even a famous (but un-named) millionaire. They settled down to a life that appeared very comfortable to a reporter from the *Western Times*:

'They occupy good quarters overlooking the River Frome, and commanding a beautiful view of the surrounding country ... They have the run of the recreation grounds, and spend much of their time in games. Most of them seem quite content with their lot, and, indeed, the Scots Fusiliers who are guarding them, are inclined to envy them. Their food is good, they have tobacco allowed them, and a small weekly sum for luxuries.'

Curious crowds gathered to watch the men being taken out for exercise. 'On Monday morning a party of about 60 of the Teutonic prisoners, under military escort, marched out into the country along Wareham road for a "constitutional",' reported the *Weymouth Telegram*.

Inside the camp life was generally harmonious, although there was the odd hiccup. According to the *Telegram*: 'An Austrian and a German engaged in a heated argument as to which country started the war. The sentries refused to interfere and the men, in order to settle their differences, had to resort to fisticuffs, the Austrian giving his burly opponent a severe hiding.'

By the end of August 1914, more than 1,000 men filled the camp's barrack buildings and so extra tents, and later huts, were erected to supplement the existing accommodation. The prison population would continue to swell as captured German soldiers began to arrive from the Front. Initially, these prisoners had been held at camps in France, but the British military authorities feared that some might attempt to escape and rejoin the fighting too easily, and it was therefore decided that they should be brought back to Britain. As a result, Dorchester's civilian internees were moved to camps elsewhere in the country and the internment camp became a military one.

German prisoners set off on a 'constitutional' in Dorchester, in a photograph thought to have been taken in August or September 1914, when most of those held were still civilians.
(Courtesy of Dr Colin Chapman).

an Prisoners
Guard, marching out.
ney, Dorchester. 19

Dorchester Prison Camp, photographed around 1915 or 1916.
(Courtesy of Dr Colin Chapman).

Local people were fascinated by the enemy soldiers and girls gathered in groups to watch them. So open were they in their admiration that, in April 1915, one correspondent wrote to the *Dorset County Chronicle* and pointedly asked 'the feather-brained daughters of Eve, who congregate about the Dorchester barracks when the German prisoners are marching out for their daily walk, to remember that they are Englishwomen'.

Great efforts were made to ensure that life in the camp was comfortable, not only to satisfy international agreements about the humane treatment of prisoners, but also to keep the dreaded 'barbed wire disease' at bay. This was the term used to describe the mental health problems that often resulted from long periods of confinement in crowded quarters with little to do.

Christmas 1916 edition of the Dorchester German prisoners' newspaper, *Deutsche Blätter*. *(Courtesy of Dr Colin Chapman).*

German prisoners pose for a photograph in front of a camp hut (note the instrument – music played a key role in the activities organised to keep prisoners occupied). *(Courtesy of Dr Colin Chapman).*

The camp was very well equipped, with its own theatre, library, reading room, chapel, and even a pets corner. Prisoners were allowed to write home twice a week (on semi-glossy paper so that invisible ink couldn't be used) and to receive unlimited mail and parcels. There was

German prisoners outside a farrier's workshop, thought to be at Dorchester. *(Courtesy of Dr Colin Chapman).*

plenty to occupy them in the camp workshops, which produced everything from mailbags (65,000 during the war) to furniture (this was sold by the Quakers, often to buyers in America in order not to upset domestic manufacturers). Sport and musical activities were encouraged and prisoners also produced their own newspaper. However, there was no escaping the regulation tunics that marked them out as prisoners, with red or blue patches sewn on to the back of their jackets.

The Dorchester camp claimed a moment of fame at the end of 1914, when a daring escape was made by one prisoner, Otto Koehn, who stowed away amongst the luggage of fellow PoWs who were being repatriated. The young German lieutenant hid in a wooden box, roughly 3ft square, equipped with food, drink and a supply of oxygen. Things went wrong at Tilbury Docks, when two crewmen tried to load the box on to a ship bound for Rotterdam. *The Times* reported:

Prisoners of War Camp,
DORCHESTER.

16th, November, 1916.

Dear Sir,

In reply to your letter of the 15th instant, if you wish to employ Prisoners of War you will have to pay the cost of their train fare from Dorchester to Upwey also the same for the escort which would be two men if you employ four Prisoners.

You would have to pay the standard rate of wages for similar work which the Labour Bureau informs me is 6d per hour.

You will also have to sign the enclosed slip signifying your agreement to the terms therein stated.

As you would have to pay the Railway fares and also provide tools for the workmen, I will, when making application to my Command Headquarters for these men to be employed, recommend that 1d per hour be deducted (from what you would have to pay) for the provision of tools & ½d per hour to help defray the cost of railway fares.

On hearing from you that you are agreeable to these terms I will put forward the application.

It usually takes 4 or 5 days to get a reply.

Yours truly,

Lt-Colonel.
Commandant.

Mr. B. Butler Bowden,
Upwey House,
Upwey,
Dorset.

A letter arranging for Dorchester prisoners of war to work at Upwey.
(Courtesy of Weymouth Library, Ref: LB/Bow BO.1).

'On account of its weight and the difficulty of handling it, these men rolled it over and over. They had just reached the gangway with the box when, to their astonishment, the lid at the side gave way and the head and arm of a man protruded from the box. "Man inside! Man inside!" they shouted.'

Koehn struggled out, dazed and unable to stand, having been doubled up inside for nearly 15 hours. The box was found to contain 'a blanket, two champagne bottles filled with water, a bottle of meat extract, and about a dozen bananas and banana skins'. Also tucked away was a rubber pillow filled with oxygen, although it did not appear to have been used. Koehn was returned to Dorchester.

During the latter part of the war, working parties from the camp were sent out into the community to bolster the local workforce, which was now woefully short of men. Prisoners were employed in road-mending, quarrying and farm work (some said the harvest couldn't have been gathered in without them) for which they were paid a wage, and they were put up in subsidiary work camps nearby.

When local employers requested PoW labour, business-like arrangements were entered into. In November 1916 the commandant at Dorchester Prison Camp, Lieutenant Colonel Bulkeley, sent this reply to Mr B. Butler Bowden, of Upwey House, Upwey:

'If you wish to employ prisoners of war you will have to pay the cost of their train fare from Dorchester to Upwey, also the same for the escort which would be two men if you employ four Prisoners.

'You would have to pay the standard rate of wages for similar work which the Labour Bureau informs me is 6d per hour.

'As you would have to pay the Railway fares and also provide tools for the workmen, I will, when making application to my Command Headquarters for these men to be employed, recommend that 1d per hour be deducted (from what you would have to pay) for the provision of tools & ½d per hour to help defray the cost of railway fares.'

Prisoners soon became a familiar sight and locals got used to noticing them out and about in the area. On Portland, between 1916 and 1918, they arrived each day at Easton Station to be marched up Reforne to Wide Street, where they were building a road. Children would run alongside the Germans, chanting the following rhyme to the tune of an old gospel hymn:

'At the cross at the cross
Where the Kaiser lost his hoss [sic]

And the Eagle on his helmet flew away,
He was eating German buns
When he heard the British guns
That frightened the Kaiser right away.'

This would prompt the warders to chase them, much to the delight of the children and amusement of the prisoners.

On the edge of Wide Street, the prisoners used a partly-finished building for their breaks and to shelter in during inclement weather. For company there was the sexton's donkey, which was stabled in a wooden outbuilding nearby. The road they built survives today as footpath No 20, which leads to the coastal footpath.

Not everyone in the area was happy about the use of German labour. Industrial unrest had been a feature of life in pre-war Britain, with workers demanding better pay and working conditions, and although strikes were banned when the conflict began, militancy still bubbled under the surface. In 1915, when new huts were being erected at the Dorchester camp, trade unions insisted that all work was carried out by British labour rather than PoWs.

In April 1917, questions were even raised in the House of Commons about PoW labour. The Home Secretary was asked by Leeds East MP James O'Grady whether he was aware that 'every morning some hundreds of German prisoners of war come into Dorchester for work at small workshops in the town'? The House was told that five Germans were employed by one small cabinet-maker, 'for a small pittance to the detriment of the wages and employment of British workmen.' Two British soldiers also remained there all day guarding the prisoners. Couldn't the prisoners be better employed on the land or on road-making, another MP asked? The Home Secretary replied that accommodation near such work sites was not yet ready and until it was, the prisoners were being allowed to work for local employers on a temporary basis, 'by the week only'.

***

By the spring of 1915 huge numbers of British and Empire troops were being killed and wounded on the Western Front, notably in battles at Neuve Chapelle and Hill 60, a strategic hilltop near Ypres in Belgium. The depressing details began filtering back to Britain through newspaper reports, which the Sneyd-Kynnersley family followed with a keen eye. Madge noted the main events at the Front in her diary, sometimes alongside domestic matters of rather less consequence:

12 April – 'Awful stories about how Neuve Chapelle was a failure and we fired on our own men. 12,000 British casualties.'

13 April – 'Went to town early with mother, bought very full "umbrella skirt", blue serge 17s 11d. Short and full. I don't like these new fashions.'

18 April – 'English captured Hill 60, a very important one and in spite of violent counter attacks held it during the week.'

27 April – 'Germans advance by means of asphyxiating gases, most cruel and illegal torture.'

The asphyxiating gas was chlorine, first introduced used as a weapon on the Western Front by the Germans in April 1915. Fired from canisters, it drifted on the prevailing wind and destroyed victims' respiratory organs, leading to slow death by asphyxiation. Scores of men from the 1st Dorsets died as the result of a gas attack while they were defending Hill 60. Many tried to escape the gas by crouching in their trenches, but the heavy vapour sank over them and rendered such attempts futile. Far better to have climbed on to the firing step – risky though that was – to stay above the level of the chlorine. An officer of the battalion inspecting the lines afterwards counted 53 dead, 206 poisoned (of whom half would not survive) and 32 missing.

As casualties mounted the call for new recruits was becoming increasingly urgent at home and the commander of the Dorset Royal Garrison Artillery, Major M. J. Raymond, put out this appeal in August:

'We are now supplying men for siege artillery. Over 100 men have already presented themselves, but I want another 150. Recruits must be prepared to serve anywhere but their training will take place in the Weymouth defences, and they are chiefly required here. I specially appeal to Dorset men to support a Dorset unit, and take their share in the defence of their own country.'

Applicants had to be at least 5ft 6in – 3 inches taller than the minimum height for ordinary infantrymen, due to the heavy work demanded by the big guns.

Appeals like Major Raymond's were designed put pressure on men who hadn't already volunteered, encouraging them to show loyalty to their King and county. But once enlisted, they became part of a military machine which had little time to consider the well-being of individuals, as the case of 20-year-old Herbert Bungay, an infantryman based at the

'Weymouth ... an ideal place for our wounded soldiers,' noted the *Nursing Times* in January 1916.
(Courtesy of Weymouth Library, Ref: L942.331 Wey.12).

Verne Citadel on Portland, shows.

In September 1915, Herbert was found dead in his bed, having shot himself. The inquest heard that there had been warning signs. According to his colleagues, Bungay, who came from Titchfield in Hampshire, had been depressed and spent most of his time reading books and magazines, having only left the barracks once since coming to Portland. Although never before in trouble, the day before his death Herbert had been fetched from his bed, after failing to turn up for guard duty, and given 'a good talking to' by the commanding officer. The inquest verdict was: 'Death from a gunshot wound, self inflicted whilst in a state of unsound mind.'

From the very outset of the war, a constant flow of casualties were evacuated to hospitals in South Dorset, initially from local army camps where accidents, illnesses and even exposure took their toll, and then from the battlefields. Beds were provided not only at existing hospitals but also in country houses converted for the purpose by their owners.

Dorset County Hospital in Dorchester offered 120 beds for wounded servicemen, whilst pledging to continue to serve the county's poor. These military beds were at the main hospital building (then off Princes Street), the Masonic Hall and Colliton House, the home of Major Denzil Hughes-Onslow and his wife Marion, a prominent county couple. Facilities at Colliton expanded during the war, with marquees erected in the surrounding park, and by 1917 the hospital accommodated 200 beds. Sadly, Major Hughes-Onslow would never again enjoy Colliton House in peace-time. Serving in France with the 6th Battalion, the Dorsetshire Regiment, he was killed by a stray bullet in 1916.

Weymouth had its share of hospitals too, including several auxiliary hospitals where soldiers were sent to recover once their wounds had been treated. Staffed mainly by Red Cross nurses, they were housed in a variety of locations. One was set up at the Convent of the Sacred Heart, in Carlton Road, where the sisters helped out as cooks. Another took over a meeting room belonging to the Girls' Friendly Society – a pioneering organisation run by women to protect young working girls. (These beds were later transferred to a larger house at Old Castle Road, overlooking the Portland Harbour, where it was known as Ryme Hospital.) The Massandra Hospital was established in a private house at Greenhill, surrounded by gardens which boasted tennis courts and croquet lawns. A fourth hospital was squeezed into a hall at St John's Mission House.

According to *The Nursing Times*, the town's seaside location made it the perfect place to convalesce:

'Weymouth, that charming South Coast town of Royal Georgian memories, with its beautiful wide bay, its sandy beach, fine esplanade, and distinction of being one of the sunniest towns in England is an ideal place for our wounded soldiers. There are no very large hospitals here but all of them are excellent ... Most of them lie very near the shore so that not only the convalescents, but many of the still quite helpless patients are able to enjoy the sunshine on the promenade. One meets them there at all hours of the day, men in hospital blue [patients' uniform] sometimes wheeling their comrades.'

Wounded servicemen were initially admitted to military hospitals for treatment, and in Weymouth, one such hospital was established at Sidney Hall, an imposing building at the foot of Boot Hill, which was swiftly converted at the outbreak of war and staffed by a mixture of professionally trained and volunteer nurses. The hall had been presented to the parish in 1895 by local brewer Sir John Groves, for use largely by

So. SYDNEY HALL So.
MILITARY HOSPITAL 1916

Sidney Hall boasted one of the largest wartime hospital wards in England. *(Courtesy of the Sandes family).*

the Church Lads' Brigade, in memory of his late son and former brigade member, Sidney. Without on-site operating theatres, staff worked in partnership with the Royal Hospital – Weymouth's free general hospital – where surgery was carried out on military patients, and civilians were also still admitted.

Sidney Hall's ground floor boasted row upon row of beds and was said to be one of the largest wards in England. An impressive sight indeed, observed *The Nursing Times*: 'The effect is most cheerful and interesting. One might think it difficult to maintain discipline and order in such a huge ward, but evidently the sisters have no such trouble here.' Those words of praise were written in January 1916, but nothing could have been further from the truth at the beginning of 1915, when a tragic incident revealed that all was not as it should have been at Sidney Hall.

The incident concerned Private James Gribbin, a 37-year-old soldier who was stationed at Chickerell Army Camp with the Royal Scots

Regiment. One night he was brought to the hospital, having been accidentally run over by a car. Semi-conscious and with an injury to his forehead, Gribbin was helped inside, complaining of pains in his legs. Instead of a doctor being sent for, however, the nurse in charge assumed that Gribbin was drunk (although there was no evidence for this). She bandaged his head and sent him back to Chickerell Camp, where he was put into the guard tent and covered with a blanket. Early the next morning he was found dead.

An inquest heard that Gribbin had suffered dreadful internal injuries which had gone undetected. 'The pelvis bone was broken into three, and there were several splinters of bone about, which showed the violence of the injury,' reported the doctor who carried out the post-mortem examination. His death had been due to shock and heart failure. A catalogue of failures at Sidney Hall were then revealed to the inquest. There was no resident medical officer or matron, instead, the matron fromWeymouth Royal Hospital 'looked in for a few hours daily'. The nurse in charge on the night in question was not fully trained. The staff who had dealt with Gribbin could hardly hear what he said, because of the level of noise and rowdiness around them. The coroner asked incredulously: 'Have you no authority? It seems extraordinary that there should have been a crowd of people in a receiving ward like this.'

The doctor who conducted the post-mortem concluded that, even if medical aid had been provided, Gribbin would still have died. Yet that was of little consolation to his friends and family, nor to those in the medical profession who felt the hospital should have done better. A highly critical article appeared in the *British Journal of Nursing*:

'Deep indignation is felt by trained nurses that a soldier suffering, according to the medical evidence, from mortal injuries, should have been sent away from the Sidney Hall Military Hospital, to which he had been taken, and without medical advice, on the assumption that he was drunk, sent back to camp, and left to die alone, lying on the ground, just covered with a blanket, in the Guard Room.

'We ask the public to judge whether the system of nursing, as exemplified in the case under consideration, is an efficient system … We ask all mothers and fathers who read the account of this case how they would feel if this poor man had been one of their own sons … Do not forget that this man was prepared to risk his life in the defence of the Empire.'

If any good came of Gribbin's terrible ordeal it was that two months later, in May 1915, the *Journal* could report that 'proper staff and trained nurses and orderlies' had been taken on at Sidney Hall.

Some of the first wounded men to arrive in Weymouth in 1914 were Belgian soldiers, who had been defending their country against the invading German Army. Many were sent to the town's Princess Christian Hospital in Melcombe Avenue, Greenhill, which was formerly a hospital for women and children.

Madge Sneyd-Kynnersley was transferred there to help nurse the Belgians and this is her account of the first day:

> 'Nursing Belgian wounded. One could talk a little English but I jabbered French to them. All from Antwerp and war, rheumatic with lying in trenches, 95 altogether about 25 in my ward. Gave them tea and supper, weak coffee … made beds, took pulses and respirations, massaged painful ankle and leg, and after went round with a nurse who did dressings, I put on bandages, one awful one on groin (disgusting) did it badly.'

THE BRITISH JOURNAL OF NURSING

And Midwife Supplement.

WITH WHICH IS INCORPORATED

THE NURSING RECORD

VOL. LIV.

JANUARY to JUNE, 1915.

London:
THE NURSING PRESS, Ltd., 431, Oxford Street, W.

The British Journal of Nursing **was highly critical of practices at Sidney Hall in a report published on 27 March 1915.** *(Reproduced by courtesy of the Royal College of Nursing).*

Many Belgians were traumatised by their experiences for, although tales of German atrocities were often exaggerated, there can be no doubt about the country's intense suffering during the invasion.

Madge became friendly with one Belgian in particular, Corporal Alphonse Bott, who confided in her about what he had been through. Alphonse wrote a poem in his native French, describing Prussian troops who were 'full of hate, like a vile pack unleashed' ransacking villages and slaughtering civilians. His own home had been set on fire by a soldier 'who left the scene with a smile', he told Madge. He had lost both his parents and his sister, and was himself was wounded by an exploding shell.

The people of Weymouth did their best to make the Belgian soldiers feel welcome. All sorts of entertainments were laid on, such as a matinee performance of *The Duke of Killiekrankie* at the Pavilion Theatre, which

Kaiser Wilhem Built a navy
But its such a sell.

(Above and below) The humorous 'Kaiser cartoons' drawn by the wounded Belgian soldier Alphonse Bott for Madge Sneyd-Kynnersley in 1914. *(Courtesy of the Sandes family).*

For all the water he has got is in the Kiel Canal

Madge described rather drily in her diary: '100 Belgians invited tho' they couldn't understand a word. Sang Tipperary hundreds of times and played Allies' national anthems. And there were messages of greeting on curtain to which the Belgians cheered and shouted and clapped.'

A few days later, Madge's diary read more touchingly: 'Great Belgian funeral, Alphonse too upset with it to come to tea.' When finally he left Weymouth, Alphonse presented Madge with an amusing souvenir. In her autograph book he draw a pair of cartoons showing the German Kaiser, a man full of naval ambitions, playing with his toy boats in the Kiel Canal. In a mocking reference to Germany's land-locked position, the caption read: 'Kaiser Wilhelm built a navy but it's such a sell, for all the water he has got is in the Kiel Canal.'

One of South Dorset's most colourful wartime episodes was the arrival of the 'Anzacs' (the Australian and New Zealand Army Corps) in Weymouth. The town became a base for wounded Antipodean soldiers, who were sent there to convalesce before being sent back to the Front or, in the worst cases, discharged and shipped home. The base opened in May 1915 and was initially for Australian and New Zealand troops, but when New Zealand opened its own depot in Essex in 1916, the Australians had Weymouth to themselves.

As the first casualties arrived from the Battle of Gallipoli in the spring of 1915, they were billeted at a muddy camp at Chickerell, previously occupied by the Royal Scots Regiment. It would become known as 'Monte Video Camp', after a large house of that name which is still standing nearby. As more and more Anzacs poured into Weymouth, new camps were opened at Westham (for soldiers who were likely to remain permanently unfit) and Littlemoor, then in 1917 a base at the Verne

Anzac troops gather at Weymouth's Alexandra Gardens for dispersal to local convalescent camps, around 1917-18.
(Courtesy of Weymouth Museum, Ref: LH/IL/CL/R/019).

Support staff for the Anzac soldiers in Weymouth pose inside the Kursaal (a covered bandstand) at Alexandra Gardens.
(Courtesy of Weymouth Museum, Ref: LH/IL/PH/EV/343).

Citadel on Portland was opened too.

Corporal Bert Smythe was among the first of the Gallipoli wounded to arrive in June 1915 and he was billeted at the Monte Video Camp. From there he wrote to his family in Australia:

'Chickerell is about 2½ miles out of Weymouth a pleasure resort on the South Coast of England. There are about 160 men here, all Austns & NZ's & we live in huts & have straw mattresses to sleep on. We have a pretty easy time of it. Do a little light marching in the morning, & a little again in the afternoon finishing about 4pm.

'We often have a good meal of fish. Anyone that cares to go down to the bay & help the fishermen to pull in their nets can have as much fish as they can carry away. We often get a dish full, & the cooks do them up for us for nothing.'

Local tradesmen were eager to take advantage of this lively new market, and in Westham Italian ice-cream sellers were soon standing on street corners, stirring their custard-like confection in large tubs for Australian soldiers to buy. Edward Samways, a boy living in Westham at the time, watched the Aussies with interest and later recalled how they would smuggle him into the cinema on Abbotsbury Road under their greatcoats.

Hundreds of Anzacs were sent to recover at the Verne Citadel's military hospital on Portland, but their pitiful state on arrival prompted the local council to complain about the way in which wounded and exhausted men were forced to walk up the steep hill, laden with heavy kit. Once tucked up in hospital beds, however, their needs were well taken care of by the Easton Ladies Working Guild, whose kindness was acknowledged in this letter by the adjutant at Verne Hospital in 1917:

> 'The Medical officer at this Depot requests me to thank you for the interest you have taken in the welfare of our boys in Hospital, and he also desires me to state that the Hospital will be quite open to you any Tuesday afternoon between the hours of 2.30pm and 4pm. I have informed the guard on the South Western Gate that you are afforded full liberty of passing through.'

The Aussies could be an unruly bunch at times and certainly didn't stand on ceremony, but their humour and familiar chat endeared them to locals. A collection of Aussie snapshots, rhymes and good wishes filled the pages of an autograph book belonging to local girl Madeline Watson, who may have worked at the Monte Video Camp. One of eight children, Maggie (as she was better known) had been a servant at the Black Dog Hotel in St Mary Street, Weymouth, before the war. Her father was an employee at the Whitehead Torpedo Works in Wyke, and her mother ran The Crown, a small pub in the town. Maggie was 19 when she was given the autograph book by her mother at Christmas 1915, and many of the entries within it were contributed by Australian soldiers.

Typical of the playful ditties the Aussies were fond of writing was this one inscribed in Maggie's book:

> 'Eleven pretty little girls
> Are working in the Crown
> So if the Anzacs want a girl
> They had better call around.'

Other rhymes were more reflective:

> 'England for rest cure
> Weymouth for pleasure
> France for a strafing
> But Australia for treasures.'

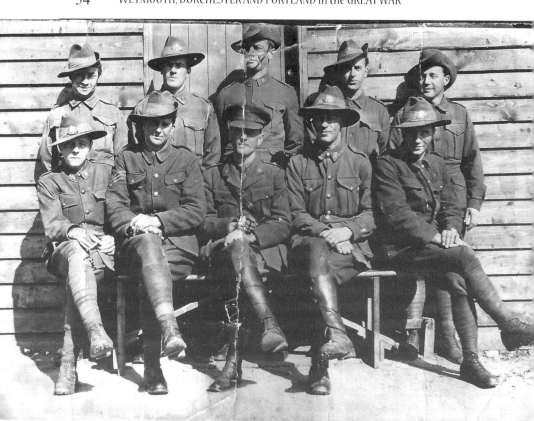

**(Opposite, above and right)
Snapshots of Anzac soldiers from
Maggie Watson's autograph book.**
*(Courtesy of Tina Morley / the Western Front
Association).*

Some men were still coming to
terms with their recent experiences
in Gallipoli and one, who signed
himself 'E.E. Haigh, 1st Battalion,
AIF', composed a verse about the
Australian Third Brigade's landing
at Anzac Cove:

'It was just break of day
As we steamed up the bay
Shot and shell all around us was
    flying
With great desperate will
We swarmed up the hill
Though we left comrades
    wounded and dying.'

Maggie's autograph book also has a
beautifully written list of 'Monte

Video Postal Staff', among whom was a soldier called Norman Pearshouse. His sketches, including one of Maggie posing elegantly with a fan, cover several pages throughout her book and he and Maggie appear to have struck up a close friendship, although both went their separate ways after the war. Maggie married in the 1920s and moved to Hong Kong with her husband, where he worked as a policeman. The couple had three sons and Maggie died in 1952. Norman is believed to have returned to Australia.

The Aussies certainly stole the hearts of many local girls during their stay in Weymouth. In a collection of memories held by Portland Heritage Trust, Mrs Ethel Braund, who was a young girl of seven when war broke out, recalled the liaisons between Portland girls and Australian troops. 'They were notorious for their "manly prowess",' she said, 'the Portland girls went down like ninepins.' Mrs Braund remembered leaning over a garden wall, 'watching Australian soldiers marching away, perhaps back to the Front or maybe home, preceded by a band and accompanied by weeping females. I didn't realise the significance of that at the time and d'you know I remember that so clearly, to such an extent that any military music now makes me cry.'

Despite Weymouth's warm welcome, many recovering Anzacs couldn't wait to return to the Front. They felt uncomfortable living 'cushy' lives in Blighty when their friends were fighting and dying on the battlefield. Among them was Fred Martin, who wrote to his father in Queensland: 'There is absolutely no news, only that I am fed up to the mouth with Weymouth.' Martin was recovering at Westham Camp after contracting typhoid in Gallipoli and he watched enviously as fellow soldiers departed for France:

'A draft left last night at about 2 o'clock in the morning … I could have howled when the band played them away. All of the boys turned out to see them off and marched with them to the station. By Jove it

A photograph of Maggie Watson at the front of her autograph book, given to her when she was 19 by her mother for Christmas 1915.

(Courtesy of Tina Morley / the Western Front Association).

A photograph thought to be of Norman Pearshouse, an Australian soldier who struck up a friendship with Weymouth girl Maggie Watson, during the war. *(Courtesy of Tina Morley / the Western Front Association).*

was lively. A great number of the chaps were in their pyjamas. The canteen had been opened for some time so that they could get a drink before they left. Of course they took the opportunity. A couple of big ambulance motor cars followed up the draft picking up the stragglers. Well I suppose they are in France now.'

Fred finally got his wish in the summer of 1916 when he returned to the Western Front, just before his twenty-first birthday, and was later promoted to lieutenant. He was killed in action in September 1917.

After a year of conflict, the novelty of war had long since worn off and life on the Home Front had become decidedly dreary. Every now

and again, however, a sensational story in the newspapers would liven up conversation at British breakfast tables, such as the scandal that erupted in early 1915 surrounding the bigamous marriage of a girl aged 16 to a man claiming to be 'the Marquis de Lafaye'. In reality, the 'Marquis' was Frank de Lafaye Biard, the 26-year-old son of a schoolmaster. He was tried at the Old Bailey and sentenced to three years' penal servitude.

Other stories were more distressing, such as the case reported in September 1915 by the *Western Gazette* under the heading, 'A Dorchester sensation – Alleged shocking depravity'. It resulted from a police raid on a house in All Saint's Road, Dorchester, which different men – mostly soldiers – had been seen frequenting during the early hours. When officers arrived with a search warrant they found two girls, aged 12 and 14, in bed with a lance corporal. Their mother was downstairs with another soldier, while her four

Drawing of Maggie Watson by Norman Pearshouse.
(Courtesy of Tina Morley / the Western Front Association).

other children slept elsewhere in the house.

The ensuing court case was unpleasant, and all females who were not directly concerned with the case were asked to leave the courtroom. The mother appeared, smartly dressed, to answer the charge of keeping a disorderly house, which she denied. The court heard that when confronted by the police, she had said the girls were not under her control and she could do nothing with them. The lance corporal had protested: 'This is all through getting into bad company. I am very sorry that I ever went to the house.' The 14-year-old said simply: 'None of this would have happened if I had a father alive. It is the way we have

Fred Martin, pictured in Australia before leaving for war: 'I am fed up with Weymouth,' he wrote while convalescing in the town.
(Courtesy of Anne McCosker).

been brought up. I am sick of this life.' Exactly what had happened to her father was not explained.

While the mother was remanded on bail to await trial, her six children, aged from seven to fourteen, were to be cared for at the local workhouse.

***

On Christmas Eve a great tea for 1,500 Anzacs was held at the Monte Video Camp, and Madge Sneyd-Kynnersley taxied over to Chickerell with her friends to help out: 'Each had 2 tables to look after and talk to men, who were awfully nice. Then walked through mud to another hut and waited for a concert which never came so we taxied home by 8.15. Anzacs sang "For they are jolly good fellows" about us.'

On this occasion the men were on their best behaviour, but only a few weeks earlier Madge had returned from a dance where she complained that the Anzacs had been 'too loving'. Such irritations were insignificant when set against the pessimism that had now set in over the prospect of a swift end to the war. Madge Sneyd-Kynnersley admitted as much when she summed up the year in her diary:

'In 1915 the European war raged in spite of all the Allies' efforts, at the end of the year we seem not much further. The Dardanelles gamble failed and the troops have now been withdrawn from Anzac [Cove] and Suvla [Bay] after most terrible loss of life among the Australians and Naval Brigade. In France there is a deadlock altho' we no longer lack ammunition, thanks to Lloyd George [Minister of Munitions David Lloyd George]. May 1916 bring peace and the desires of all our hearts (as I said in last year's diary).'

Chapter Three

1916 – SHORTAGES AND CONSCRIPTION CAUSE HARDSHIP AT HOME

'LET 'EM HAVE it, we'll show 'em!' It was a cry that could have come from any Tommy advancing across No Man's Land towards enemy trenches, but in fact it was uttered by a vengeful 'rag and bone' dealer making his rounds on Portland in January 1916.

James Miller had decided to get his own back on locals when they complained about his noisy shouts for trade, and off he set through the streets, with his assistant in tow, making as much racket as possible. After being chased down by a local policeman he ended up in court, where one witness reported that Miller 'shouted in a horrible "sing song" voice, and it was the opinion all over the island that such a practice ought to be stopped'. Miller, from Wyke, was fined 15 shillings, under a county by-law, for 'shouting to the annoyance of the public'.

While people like James Miller indulged in petty squabbles, the majority longed for a respite from conflict – for the war was taking its toll on everyone home. Fear for the safety of loved ones who were away fighting at the Front was all-pervasive, but other obstacles interrupted the smooth-running of normal life too. For instance, there was considerable disruption to train services because of troop movements, and the lack of horses made getting around difficult.

The Government's Defence of the Realm Act, introduced in 1914, was beginning to control public life in ways never seen before. When the British penchant for drinking was deemed to be costing factories too many days of lost production, DORA was used to reduce pub opening hours, weaken the strength of beer, and prohibit the buying of rounds, or 'treating' as it was known.

Shortages of goods in the shops and rising prices put a burden on families, as William Swailes, who was a boy on Portland during the war, recalled: 'Many's the time we were sent out to bring in dried cow's dung so we could have a fire, and many's the time we picked the tops off nettles to eat. They were very bad days.'

Long queues outside shops would become common, as people struggled to get hold of staples like sugar, and women cannily passed

Women were encouraged to make sure their families had a healthy diet, despite rising prices. 'Buy only meat which is nourishing,' advised an article the *Southern Times*.

their babies around to help each other get preferential treatment in food queues. Margarine was starting to be used as an alternative to butter, bread contained potato flour when grain was in short supply, and fresh meat was increasingly hard to obtain. Oxo placed advertisements in the local press with recipes for nourishing vegetarian meals such as cabbage and chestnuts, or carrots with fine herbs, helpfully explaining: 'Oxo can be used in conjunction with potatoes and other vegetables to make many inexpensive dishes which take the place of a meat course.'

An article in the *Southern Times* urged women not to neglect their families' health in the face of rising prices:

> 'Doubtless everyone has cut down the breakfast and dinner menus for many months past. It must be done, incomes decrease, but foodstuffs are becoming dearer and somehow bills have to be kept normal … You should determine to buy only that meat which is nourishing, and which can be used up to the last degree. Then your butcher's bill need not be exorbitantly high, and your family will not suffer from weakened constitutions, poor blood and bad nerves.'

From time to time comestibles were washed up on Dorset beaches from ships that had been sunk by enemy submarines in the English Channel. This was too good an opportunity to miss for local boys like William Swailes:

> 'When we used to go down to our bathing spots we were finding bags of flour and the fishermen down at Balaclava, who'd seen them for weeks, said if you cut the bag open and pull away the dough, you got good flour. So we were never short of flour in our house, or tins of milk which came floating in as well.'

Sadly, not all schoolboy salvage expeditions ended happily. One day a Portland headmaster recorded in his daily log the absence of several pupils, who had been 'away getting wreckage which has been

The war had become part of everyday life for schoolchildren like these, in Dorset and across the country. *(Courtesy of Frenchay Village Museum).*

plentiful on the shores this week. One lad walked out to sea and drowned.'

Coal for domestic use was scarce because priority was given to supplying the war effort, particularly the manufacture of munitions, the transport of troops, and the fuelling of ships. The headmaster of Grove Infant School on Portland wrote in his log one winter's day: 'On two mornings this week the gas was lit for one hour in big room, the temperature only being 36 [2 degrees centigrade]. The east end of the room being so cold the classes were grouped more or less together so as to be near the fire at the west end.'

On the registers at Grove School were the children of many staff at Portland Prison. The school was divided into three sections: one for infants, one for girls, and one for boys. Extracts from the daily logs for 1916 suggest the youngsters were used to the war being part of their lives:

19 March (Infants' school): 'Miss Magawley, Supplementary

Teacher, left at 2.45 every afternoon this week to do hospital work in Weymouth. Girls from Girls School helped with Babies Class.'

12 May (Boys' school): 'Kelly and Phelan [pupils] have passed as boys for the Army and come irregularly.'

31 October (Girls' school): 'School will be closed at 3.30pm during the months of November, December and January. This is to prevent lighting and to allow caretaker to clean school before dark during the war.'

28 November (Girls' school): 'Received wool from the "War Distress Committee" to give children to make socks for soldiers. These will be partly made during the needlework lesson and finished at home.'

21 December (Boys' school): 'Received a visit from Sgnt H White an old boy and once a monitor who left 23 years ago. He has won the DCM and Military Medal in the war.'

Elsewhere on Portland, pupils at St George's Infants School were encouraged to save up to buy 'comforts' for troops at the Front and in German prison camps. In return, letters like this one were sent thanking the children, albeit rather formally:

'Received your most welcome parcel of cigarettes and tobacco. They will go a long way to lighten our long hours in the trench and billets. Trust the British soldier to win a decisive victory of the Huns. Wishing you every success in your studies. We remain Signal Section, 1st Battalion, Gordon Highlanders, 8th Brigade, 3rd Division, British Forces, France.'

One of the most profound ways in which war affected people's lives in 1916 was the introduction of conscription. After an initial rush of volunteers, the number of new army recruits soon began dwindling, particularly in Weymouth. This rather pithy observation by Madge Sneyd-Kynnersley showed that people had been well aware of the problem as early as October 1915: 'Recruiting meeting in Alexandra Gardens – Patriotic band, speeches by Gens Pink and Johnson and the Mayor etc. They got about 10 recruits, including a policeman and an old man from Co-operative Stores with 2 sons fighting.'

With casualties growing and too few coming forward at home to replace them, the Government decided it had no choice but to make enlistment compulsory. Initially only single men between the ages of 18 and 41 were called up, unless they were widowed with children

A scene from the Battle of Passchendaele, fought on the Western Front, during which Weymouth conscript Ernest Patterson lost his life in August 1917. *(Courtesy of Taylor Library).*

or ministers of religion. But in May 1916 married men also became liable for the call-up.

Who could blame men for not wanting to go and fight, though – especially those with families? The reality of war was now clear for all to see in newspaper reports, from tales told by servicemen who came home on leave or wounded, and even in cinemas where newsreels were showing footage of fighting.

Ernest Patterson from Emmadale Road in the Westham area of Weymouth, held out until 1917 when he was forced to join the army. Until then he had worked as a butcher's boy and was known as a happy-go-lucky young man, who enjoyed a pint and could often be seen cycling home from work, weaving rather erratically along the road. Ernest had a wife and a young daughter, who was just three years old when he left for the Western Front. Two weeks after arriving in France he was killed at Passchendaele in August 1917, aged 27. His body was never found and his name is remembered on the Tyne Cot Memorial in Belgium.

Those who objected to being sent to fight could have their appeals heard by local military tribunals, but like most reluctant conscripts Ernest probably didn't consider applying for an exemption simply because so few were granted. His grandson, Richard Samways, recalled:

'It was his sister who many years later told me of his great reluctance to join up ... and also of his fondness for a pint and the wobbly bicycle ride home.'

The grounds for exemption from military service were stringently enforced and included: business or domestic hardship; medical unfitness; being employed in work of national importance; and conscientious objection. Dorset's Military Service Tribunal sat regularly in different parts of the county, listening carefully to the cases that came before them. Men who argued that their absence would create difficulties for their families or businesses were often granted temporary exemptions of between a few weeks and six months, so that alternative arrangements could be made.

Despite their reputation for strictness, some tribunals were reasonably sympathetic. In December 1916 the Dorset panel considered the case of Weymouth builder Walter King, 40, who was in partnership with his 70-year-old father. The military authorities wanted King to go and fight and leave his father to take care of business, even though much of the work involved climbing on to roofs for repair work. The tribunal, however, said that no 70-year-old man should be expected to clamber around on roofs, and granted King a temporary exemption.

They were rather less patient with John Churchouse, 37, who was described as 'a grocer, greengrocer, journeyman butcher, and the only tripe dresser in Weymouth'. He had already been granted an exemption until 31 December 1916, yet appealed for an extension, saying that if he had to leave by the end of the year it would cause great hardship. 'There is hardship everywhere. I do not see exactly how time will help a man in your position,' replied the chairman tersely. 'But you will have exemption until 31 January.'

With army camps dotted all over the countryside, the military was now part of everyday life. 'Watched soldiers in fields learning to salute, hold rifles and fling themselves flat on the ground after running. Funny,' observed an amused Madge Sneyd-Kynnersley, as she looked out at them from the window of the Weymouth hospital where she worked as a Red Cross nurse. Her sister Sylvia also noticed signs of army training during an evening stroll on the edge of town: 'Kitty and I went for a very long walk, Radipole and home through Westham golf links. Many fortifications and earth works for guns there.'

The gathering of so many men in concentrated areas inevitably led to a certain amount of rowdiness, and local magistrates were never short of 'drunk and disorderly' cases during the war years. Most soldiers favoured a trip to the pub when they were off-duty, but there were alternatives. The Temperance movement had grown rapidly during the Victorian era and now ran organisations like the Soldiers' Home and Institute in Dorchester, which offered a coffee bar and reading room at its premises in North Square, as well as bathrooms and a library – all alcohol-free. The YMCA and Salvation Army set up their own huts at local army camps, which were popular with the men and served as hubs for recreation and camp entertainment.

Theatres proved a big attraction too, especially in Weymouth where such facilities had always been on hand for holidaymakers. The Pavilion, an elegant wooden structure next to the pier, advertised a varied programme ranging from musical revues, like the funny but rather vulgar *Fine Feathers*, to lectures such as one delivered in broken English by a Russian exile called Alexis Aladin. The Pavilion had faced an uncertain future at the outbreak of war when, in September 1914, the town council had decided to close it. Not only did members feel it was inappropriate to be running such a place of entertainment during wartime, they were also concerned that it might become a target for enemy airships.

Early stars like Charlie Chaplin drew in large audiences at picture houses in Dorset and across the country during the war.

Before the theatre could be completely closed down, however, Ernest Wheeler, a prominent businessman in the town, offered to rent it, with an initial lease of six months for £200. In fact, Ernest ran the theatre throughout the conflict and continued to do so until the outbreak of the Second World War.

Picture houses were becoming more and more popular too, showing the latest silent films featuring early stars like Charlie Chaplin and Mary Pickford. Particularly celebrated early in the war was a Chaplin film called *Charlie at the Bank*. Young George Formby, who would make a name for himself entertaining troops during the Second World War, had just made his screen debut in *By the Shortest of Heads*, which was shown at the Weymouth Palladium in May 1916. 'Very good racing picture – thrilling,' wrote one local reviewer.

Some men still preferred an evening in the pub though, and the sight of tipsy Australian servicemen toppling into Weymouth harbour as they left the inns around Hope Square at closing time, often provided amusement for locals – until tragedy struck. One stormy night in early January, the body of an Australian soldier was pulled from the harbour and carried into the nearby George Inn, where for over an hour efforts were made to revive him, to no avail. The inquest into the death of Private Herbert Butterworth, 33, heard that he had not been drinking and the accident was more likely to have happened because the harbour was in darkness, due to military lighting restrictions.

During the next nine days, three more bodies were pulled from the harbour: a New Zealand soldier and two locals, a servant girl, and a seaman. Once again, poor lighting was blamed. At one of the inquests a juror exclaimed: 'It is bad enough for townspeople but what must it be like for the thousands of military men, strangers, who come to the town?' The coroner had some stern words too: 'I think our harbour has been very, very dangerous lately. It is not the town. It is the military authorities who have given us instructions to put the lights out.' As a result, the lighting around the harbour was improved.

While many Antipodean servicemen enjoyed a few pints, by and large, without complaint from local residents, drunkenness elsewhere was more problematic. Young William Swailes witnessed the way in which the hard-drinking troops of the King's Own Scottish Borderers filled locals with fear, when they were stationed on Portland. He recalled:

'Mum and Dad and we children had to walk from Augusta Road right the way down to Fortuneswell where we were registered for meat. That would be about eight miles and we would have to do it sometimes in the evenings when my father was off duty. We used to walk across the old quarries, down the Incline and into Fortuneswell to buy the little bit of meat that we were allowed. We were often accosted by these soldiers coming back from the pub in the Grove at night. They were drunk and we were quite fearful of the situation.'

Worse still were the soldiers who created fear in the families with whom they were billeted. Ethel Braund was seven when war broke out and she lived with her family at Reforne on Portland. She remembered her mother being ordered to take in men of the Royal Naval Division:

'Ours was one of the few houses that had a bathroom and they wanted mother to take an officer. She said she couldn't undertake to look after an officer, she didn't realize he'd have his own servant to look after him and she thought she would have to look after him. She'd got a big family of small children at the time so they, very meanly, billeted the three roughest men in the lot – and they were a rough lot – on her. I remember them; I remember them, they were terrible.'

The Royal Naval Division was formed at the beginning of the war to soak up a surplus of some 20,000-30,000 Royal Navy reservists who could not be found jobs in the fleet. The division served on land, alongside the army, and in the spring of 1915 it was involved in the Gallipoli landings. Before departing for the Mediterranean, the men of the RND were billeted with families in Portland, Plymouth and Portsmouth, while their new base was being built at Blandford Racecourse in North Dorset.

Thankfully, not all of them proved to be such unwelcome guests. One serviceman, who signed himself S.J. James, kept in touch with his Portland hosts, a Mr and Mrs Otter, long after he had departed Britain. In November 1915 he wrote to them from Gallipoli, where the weather was turning nasty and the Allies were facing defeat. In a few weeks they would evacuate the peninsula:

'Just a line to wish you all a Merry Xmas and a Happy New Year. We shall be up in the trenches on Xmas day but we hope to have as good a time as possible under the present circumstances on New Year's Day when we shall be in our rest camp. I am in pretty good health just now and hope you are all in the best of health too … I wish we were all there at Portland again having a good time billeted with you, but alas that will never be for poor Fred has gone under.

'My old bike still goes A1 but I doubt if you would recognize it or me now for we are both sadly the worse for wear. My back still gives me a lot of trouble and it will never be right till I get the bullet taken out.

'It is bitterly cold out here now and of course it will be worse when our winter really starts in January. There are very few of our old hands left now, and only one I can really call a chum. Again wishing you all the compliments of the season.'

Howe Battalion,
R.N.D.,
British Med. Exp. Force.
25:11:15

Dear Mr. and Mrs. Biles,

Just a line to wish you all a Merry Xmas and a Happy New Year.

We shall be in the trenches on Xmas day but we hope to have as good a time as possible under the present circumstances on new Years Day when we shall be in our Rest Camp. (?)   I am in pretty good health just now and hope you are all in the best of health too.   Arthur left here on a hospital ship with our Colonel, who has got typhoid and he may manage to get to England as he is the Colonel's servant.

I wish we were all three at Portland again having a good time like tea with you, but alas that will never be for poor Fred has gone under.

My old bike still goes a.1. but I doubt if you would recognise it or me now for we are both sadly the worse for wear.

My back still gives me a lot of trouble and it will never be right till I get the bullet taken out.

It is bitterly cold out here now and of course it will be worse when our winter really starts in January.   There are very few of our old hands left now and only one whom I can really call a chum.

Again wishing you all the Compliments of the season.

Yours very sincerely,
S. J. James

'I wish we were all there at Portland again,' wrote S. J. James to his former hosts. *(Courtesy of Weymouth Museum, Ref: LH/WA/092).*

One of the Royal Naval Division's most famous sons was the handsome war poet Rupert Brooke, who had enjoyed holidays in the Dorset area during his youth. Brooke died en route to Gallipoli from septicaemia, which had developed from an infected mosquito bite. Such an untimely death at the age of 27 contributed to his already growing celebrity and Madge Sneyd-Kynnersley listed a book of his poems among the presents she received on her twenty-fifth birthday in May 1916. 'Mother gave me lovely writing case, seal morocco, Kitty "Rupert Brooke's Poems" and a blue hanky, Sylvia a hair prong, Rosie a work basket.'

The book was probably *1914 and Other Poems*, which was published just after Brooke's death in April 1915 and was so popular that it had already reached its twenty-fourth reprint by 1918. Included in it was his much-loved sonnet 'The Soldier', with the opening lines:

'If I should die, think only this of me:
That there's some corner of a foreign field
That is forever England.'

***

The year 1916 is remembered particularly for two great battles, both of which would resonate deeply in South Dorset. The first was an Allied offensive intended to end the stalemate on the Western Front. The Battle of the Somme was launched on 1 July and dragged on for five months, until torrential November rain had turned the battlefield into a

'Mother gave me lovely writing case, Kitty "Rupert Brooke's Poems" and a blue hanky,' wrote Madge Sneyd-Kynnersley on 7 May 1916. *(Courtesy of the Sandes family).*

War poet Rupert Brooke, whose untimely death contributed to his celebrity.

quagmire. This was the first offensive to rely on the volunteers of Kitchener's Army, rather than the regulars of the British Army whose ranks had been so decimated. In total the British, French and German armies suffered 1,265,000 casualties, although neither side made any significant gains.

The early days of the Somme offensive were recorded in a ground-breaking British documentary, which reached cinema screens in August 1916. A silent black and white film, it depicted trench warfare, marching infantry, artillery firing on German positions, and even dead and wounded troops from both sides. In its first six weeks it was watched by 20 million people, including hundreds in Weymouth. This is how it was reviewed by the *Western Gazette*:

'Few people in Weymouth missed seeing the great cinema film of the battle of the Somme, which has caused much sensation wherever it has been shown, and which Mr Albany Ward screened at the Palladium in the latter part of last week and at the Jubilee Hall on Sunday night. On each occasion there were large audiences, the vast area of the Jubilee Hall, at the closing exhibition, being simply crowded. The wonderful preparations and the pictures of the actual fighting were viewed with intense interest, for the scenes portrayed form, as Mr Lloyd George has said, "an epic of self-sacrifice and gallantry".'

In contrast, the Battle of Jutland – the only major sea battle of the war – lasted just one day when, on 31 May 1916, the British Grand Fleet and German High Seas Fleet squared up to each other in the North Sea. The battle scenes were confused and terrifying, with visibility obscured by the black smoke discharged from thundering guns and pouring from the ships' coal boilers. One survivor wrote: 'The sea was white with fountains, kicked up by big German shells. There didn't seem room for a ship to escape.'

The British fleet lost three of its giant battlecruisers, HMS *Indefatigable*, *Queen Mary* and *Invincible* – ships that had drawn gasps from onlookers in Weymouth Bay before the war. Deep below their decks were gangs of stokers who worked relentlessly, stripped to the waist in the searing heat, shovelling coal into rows of boilers. Among *Queen Mary*'s stokers were two Dorchester men, Walter Smith and Frederick Wills. Smith, 25, had begun his working life as a gardener alongside his father and joined the navy at the age of 18. Frederick Wills, 26, had been a farm labourer before joining the navy in 1913, just before his twenty-fourth birthday. Down inside the ship, neither man would

The giant battlecruiser HMS *Queen Mary*, around 1914, and (inset) after being hit during the Battle of Jutland. She sank with the loss of 1,226 men, among them Dorchester stokers Walter Smith and Frederick Wills. (Right) How the battle was reported in Britain.
(Courtesy of the Taylor Library).

NAVAL BATTLE OFF JUTLAND.

BATTLE-CRUISER SQUADRON ENGAGED.

HEAVY LOSSES IN SHIPS AND MEN.

Five Cruisers Sunk, Another Abandoned.

EIGHT DESTROYERS LOST.

ENEMY LOSE 2 BATTLESHIPS AND BATTLE-CRUISER.

Light Cruiser, 6 Destroyers, and Submarine also Sunk.

have known much about it when the German battlecruiser *Derfflinger* began firing on the *Queen Mary*. The first shell struck one or both forward magazines, which broke the ship in two; another resulted in an explosion, causing the aft section to roll over and sink. Walter and Frederick were among the 1,266 crew who subsequently perished.

The wreck of the *Queen Mary* now lies on the bed of the North Sea and is a protected military site. Although the Battle of Jutland lasted just one day, it levied a heavy toll on both sides: the British lost 6,094 men and 14 ships; the Germans 11 ships and 2,551 men.

Madge Sneyd-Kynnersley first heard of the battle two days later, when she was staying with her sisters in Exeter:

> 'Went to Hippodrome, good show. On coming out heard terrible
> news of great naval battle (Wednesday night) in North Sea. *Queen
> Mary*, *Invincible*, *Defence*, *Indefatigable* blown up, nearly all lives
> lost and 9 destroyers – German losses unknown. Terrible news and
> so awfully worried and miserable. Awake nearly all night.'

Madge had good reason to be worried, as Lieutenant Commander
Spencer Russell, the Weymouth officer she would eventually marry, had
been involved the battle, commanding the destroyer HMS *Munster*.
During the next few days all Madge could do was follow the news
nervously. 'Papers a bit more hopeful. German losses believed large,'
she wrote, then on the following day:

> 'Wet day. Heard survivors were to spend an hour in [Exeter] station
> on way to Plymouth so Sylvia and I went and talked and took
> cigarettes. They very pleased with battle, say we have sunk about
> 30 ships – it was Hell and they had narrowest escapes. Our fleet has
> done splendidly.'

The next day Madge caught the train home, where she learned to her
relief that Spencer's family had received a wire, notifying them that he
was safe but shaken: 'Spencer was in thick of battle and thought every
moment would be his last,' she wrote.

A lesser-known theatre of the Great War that will be forever linked to
Dorset is Mesopotamia, which lies in modern-day Iraq. Here a mixed
British and Indian force, known as the Mesopotamian Expeditionary
Force, landed early in the war to protect oil supplies which were being
threatened by the Turkish Ottoman Empire, an ally of Germany. The
force included men of the Second Battalion, the Dorsetshire Regiment,
who had been based in India before the war.

During the spring of 1915, the British advanced north along the River
Tigris with the goal of capturing Baghdad. Before this prize could be
achieved, an unexpected defeat at Ctesiphon forced a retreat as far as the
Arab town of Kut-al-Amara. There, trapped on a loop of the River Tigris,
they waited until reinforcements could be sent up-river. This proved
impossible against mounting Turkish resistance and so began a siege on 5
December 1915, which would end in humiliating surrender the following
April. British captives were marched across the desert to prison camps, the
NCOs and soldiers suffering barbaric treatment at the hands of the Turks.
Only 70 of the 350 Dorsets captured survived to the Armistice.

News of the surrender at Kut was widely reported in Britain and locals immediately set to work raising money to buy 'comforts' for the men of the 2nd Dorsets in prison camps. Fundraising days were held in Dorchester, Weymouth and Bridport and by the end of 1916 more than £1,600 had been raised, to be spent on supplies like sugar, tea, tobacco and clothing. Delivery had to be delayed until it could be discovered exactly where the men were being held, and the first parcels finally left Dorchester in March 1917. Further shipments continued to be sent until the end of the war, using money raised by flag days and church collections.

A leaflet advertising a Kut Fund Day held in Dorchester on 26 July 1916 urged the public: 'Loosen your purse strings and show your patriotism.' The aim, it explained, was 'to send succour to very gallant men who capitulated to FAMINE, not to the FOE.' These words gave a hint of the deprivations the men had endured throughout the siege. The horrendous conditions at Kut-al-Amara were explained in full by Captain Warren Sandes, a member of the Mesopotamian Expeditionary Force, in letters to his mother Grace, who lived in Alexandra Road, Weymouth.

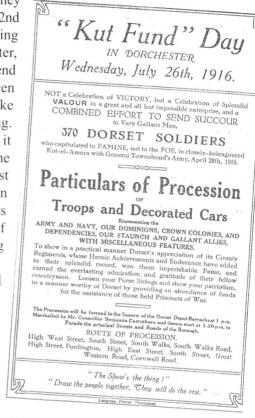

Programme of events for Dorchester's Kut Fund Day on 26 July 1916, featuring 'A Procession of Troops and Decorated Cars'.

Warren Sandes, 35, was a regular soldier with the Royal Engineers and had been based in India before the war. A keen photographer, he kept a camera to hand throughout his time in the Middle East and his rolls of film capture haunting scenes of life under siege, including several now rare shots showing men of the 2nd Dorsets.

During the siege, Sandes wrote regular letters to his mother, a former army wife herself, and although none were sent because no mail was allowed out of Kut, Sandes saved them all in the form of a journal. One of the first, dated 26 December 1915, was written just after the siege began and reflected a general feeling that the situation was temporary and relief would soon arrive:

'My dearest Mother,

'I am starting this letter now not because there is any chance of posting it yet but because things are looking more hopeful, and because there is so much to write that I am afraid I shall never be able to remember it all if I leave it late. Perhaps there will be a chance of posting it in a fortnight or so, at least we all hope so.'

In the following weeks it became obvious that relief was not on the horizon – an unhappy state of affairs, because food stocks were dwindling, dysentery caused by unclean water was beginning to take its toll, and the attacking Turks never let their captives rest.

Sandes was recovering from a fever when he wrote on 4 January 1916:

'My Dearest Mother,

'On New Year's night at dinner all were fairly cheerful except myself, till towards the end of dinner the dull distant boom of a big gun was heard. All talking stopped at once while we waited for the whistle. It came in a couple of seconds, rose to a roar, and finished with a crash in the next house [the men had taken over Arab homes]. A sergeant came running in to say that 2 sepoys [Indian soldiers] were killed and 5 wounded. This was unfortunately true, and threw a gloom over the rest of the meal.'

Captain Warren Sandes, of the Royal Engineers, wrote to his mother in Weymouth while trapped in the siege of Kut-al-Amara.

(Courtesy of the Sandes family).

By February, the weather had begun to deteriorate and the men, now weak from hunger, had resorted to eating their horses:

'We are having very cold weather. Yesterday the lowest temperatures showed 11 degrees of frost and there was ice on the small puddles at 8am. The roads are so damp and we get so little sun shut up in the town that my feet are always cold, with the result I have many chilblains on the soles of my feet and find walking very painful in spite of enormous boots. I am longing for the time when it will get a little warmer. Life is deadly monotonous ... For

Photographs taken by Captain Sandes showing men of the 2nd Dorsets under siege at Kut-al-Amara, during divine service in the trenches and manning the Front Line. *(Courtesy of The Sandes family).*

Haunting scenes of life under siege, captured on film by Captain Warren Sandes: doctors at work in a makeshift operating theatre, and emaciated Indian soldiers resting on blankets in the sun.
(Courtesy of the Sandes family).

three days we have now been living on horse and I am surprised how good it is with a little sauce to help. Butter is scarce so is not allowed for lunch or dinner. Sugar has run out altogether.'

With starvation threatening, the British were finally forced to surrender on 28 April 1916. Since the siege began, Grace Sandes had not heard from her son, and therefore it was a huge relief when she received the following telegram from the War Office: 'Regret to inform you Basra reports May 27th Captain EWC Sandes RE presumed prisoner of war.' (Captain Warren Sandes' story will be continued in Chapter Five.)

Back in Weymouth, on 30 April, Madge Sneyd-Kynnersley reported news of the surrender at Kut in her usual matter of fact way:

'Fall of Kut. Gen Townsend, after being besieged since Dec, had to surrender to Turks, all attempts at Relief having failed ... Lovely day. Lunch at Courtneys and P & J came home with me. Supper with Mrs Onslow. We played Racing Patience.'

'Regret to inform you' – the telegram sent to Grace Sandes in Weymouth, informing her of her son Warren's capture.
(Courtesy of the Sandes family).

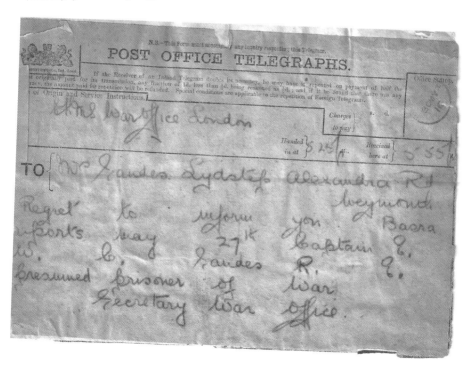

Two days earlier, Madge had noted in her diary that Anzac soldiers from the local Weymouth camps had been sent to Ireland 'to put down rebels'. While Britain had been concentrating on the Great War, Irish Republicans had re-ignited their struggle for home rule with an armed insurrection during Easter week. Despite the British Army's sparse military presence, the insurrection was quickly suppressed and its ringleaders were court-martialled and executed.

Others were imprisoned and some were sent to HM Prison Portland, where their arrival was watched by nine-year-old Mary Bool:

'One day I was down the yard and was watching prisoners being unloaded. One of them was a member of the Plunkett family, a leader of the rebellion. They were difficult prisoners and the guards had quite a lot of trouble with them. When they were coming off the ship's cutters and whalers and up onto Camber Pier, one of them got up on one of the bollards and sang "Danny Boy" and there was loud cheering and hurrah-ing and all sorts. They were marched away up to the prison, and all night long they would be calling out from their cells to one another and keeping people awake singing Irish songs. Our home was about half a mile from the prison but, if the wind was in the south-east, we could hear them plainly. One of them, maybe the one who stood on the bollard in the dockyard had a very good voice, a tenor.'

After two years of war with seemingly little progress, the people of Dorset had begun to wonder not when the conflict would end but if it would ever cease. By now few families had escaped the loss of friends or relatives and fear was something they were learning to live with. This brief newspaper story from December 1916 summed up the desperation felt by many:

'Mr and Mrs Simmons, of Franchise-street, Weymouth, are concerned about their two sons. One was a boatswain's mate on the S.S. *Britannic* which was recently mined and sunk in the Aegean Sea. Another, the eldest son, was on the *Braemar Castle*, also sunk in the Mediterranean last week. No information has been received concerning either of the two sons.'

Yet life went on, with people taking comfort in local concerns and events, which gave them something else to think about aside from the awful war. As Christmas approached in 1916, the *Western Gazette*'s local news columns for Dorchester had a reassuringly familiar feel:

Performances of 'The Messiah'

'Two performances, afternoon and evening, of Handel's "Messiah" were given at the Corn Exchange on Friday by the combined choirs of Holy Trinity Church and the Dorchester Madrigal Society, augmented by several military vocalists. The attendance in the afternoon was only moderate, but in the evening the hall was filled to overflowing and many were unable to obtain admission.'

Christmas Holidays

'At a meeting of the Dorchester Chamber of Commerce it has been recommended that the Christmas holidays should extend from Monday [Christmas Day] to Wednesday, the shops to re-open on Thursday the 28th and close again at one pm for the usual half-holiday.'

Accident to Mr Alfred Pope

'Many readers will regret to hear that Mr Alfred Pope [a well-known businessman] met with a serious accident while out shooting on Thursday. Owing to the slippery state of the hard and frosty ground he had a sharp fall and broke one of his ankles.'

The weather had been causing problems in Wyke Regis too, disrupting local football fixtures:

Football Match

'An important Garrison League match, arranged for Saturday last, between the local Whiteheads [a team from the local torpedo works] and the RGA [Royal Garrison Artillery] was unfortunately postponed owing to the extraordinary wintry conditions, which prevented the game being played. Owing to Christmas leave the match will not be played till early in the New Year.'

Although League matches were suspended during the war, football was an enormously popular participation sport at the Front, at home, and even amongst women. Keenly fought matches were played between civilian teams like Whitehead's and locally-based military sides like the Royal Garrison Artillery, and were encouraged by the Dorset Football Association. The organization had suspended competitive club football in the county for the duration, believing it to be 'the duty of every player of "football age" to help the country in its hour of need to bring the war to a successful conclusion'. Efforts had been made, however, 'to keep the game going among the large number of military stationed in the county' and, in addition, footballs had been sent to various battalions of the Dorchester Regiment serving abroad, 'from whom appreciative replies have been received'.

***

On the face of it, Christmas 1916 was celebrated in the usual way. There were generous gifts for the wounded in hospitals, where wards were decorated with festive trimmings; local clergymen dusted off the church crib and prepared their Christmas services; and in the shops trade was brisk, thanks in no small part to families buying presents for their men at the Front.

Wounded servicemen at hospitals like the Princess Christian Hospital in Weymouth celebrated Christmas with decorations and gifts generously donated by the public. *(Courtesy of the Sandes family).*

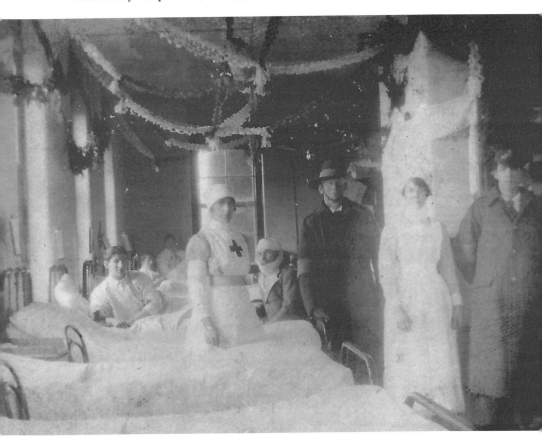

Father Xmas—Postman.

The boys at the Front need pens. They must have the best, and that is

Waterman's (Ideal) FountainPen

3 Types: Regular, **10/6** and upwards; New Lever Pocket Self-Filling and Safety Types, **15** - and upwards. (Ask about the pens with Regimental Badges and Ships' Crests.) Of Stationers and Jewellers. Booklet free from

L. G. SLOAN, Ltd., The Pen Corner,

Kingsway, London.

Only the best for the 'boys at the Front': newspaper adverts like this one in December 1916 kept trade in the shops brisk.
(Courtesy of Bristol Reference Library).

Newspaper advertisements were full of suggestions as to how the public could part with its money. One advert by the British-American Tobacco Company showed a Tommy trying to stay warm next to a brazier, while thinking about his family at home. 'Christmas is near, what shall I send him?' the caption asks. The answer: 'Cigarettes, direct from factory to soldiers at the Fronts – Christmas card enclosed with each parcel.' Another advertisement insisted: 'The boys at the Front need pens. They must have the best, and that is Waterman's Ideal Fountain Pen.'

As far as the *Western Gazette*'s correspondent in Weymouth was concerned, however, the celebrations were just a veneer concealing a nationwide depression that even festivities couldn't lift:

'So quiet a Christmas as that which has just passed has never been known in Weymouth before. There was little or no Christmas music to be heard, the railway traffic was to a considerable extent restricted, and although there was every sign that a good amount of trade was done at the business establishments of the town, there was altogether a lack on heartiness.'

The journalist continued:

'The pall of the war cloud hung heavily over the neighbourhood and the seasonal rejoicings, limited as they had necessarily to be, were mingled with expressions of hope for a speedy and victorious release from the anxieties and troubles which are oppressing the nation.'

Chapter Four

1917 - ALL HANDS TO THE PUMP FOR THE WAR EFFORT!

'IT'S OUR FLAG. Fight for it. Work for it!' These stirring words were used on posters produced by the Parliamentary Recruiting Committee in 1915, which were pasted up in community halls, on lamp posts, in working men's clubs and on street corners. They became well-known to the British public, although by 1917 this was a message that hardly needed repeating. Most people were willing to do their bit for King and country, not just at the Front but at home too, and the country had been transformed into a workshop for the war effort. Even the rural backwaters played their part.

On rough heathland to the east of Dorchester, for example, an extensive network of trenches was excavated in 1917 to help train men in the use of a secret new weapon: the tank. This machine had been invented to break the stalemate on the Western Front and it could cross trenches, survive machine gun fire and act as a shield for the infantry. Tanks first saw action during the Battle of the Somme in September 1916 and, although early models weren't always reliable, their potential was clear to see. The British Army immediately placed large orders for more, which meant a bigger training site was needed to replace the original Suffolk centre.

Secrecy was the watchword during the tank's development, hence the deliberately perplexing name of the machine, which was chosen in preference to 'container' and 'cistern'. The further they were kept from prying eyes the better, and for this reason the isolated and sparsely populated heathland around Bovington – where an infantry training camp already existed – was ideal. An added bonus was that it resembled the

This patriotic poster, produced by the Parliamentary Recruiting Committee in 1915, was familiar to every Briton by 1917 and its message hardly needed repeating.
(Courtesy of Weymouth Museum, Ref: LH/WA/029.)

The tank's arrival in Dorset was shrouded in secrecy: in this grainy newspaper shot a consignment awaits shipment to France at Avonmouth Docks. *(Courtesy of www.shirehamptonbookofremembrance.webs.com).*

type of landscape troops would soon encounter. 'The wooded country around Bovington is particularly adapted to the training of tank battalions, the rolling downs, the wood and the small streets being very similar to and as equally deserted as the battlefields of France,' said Lieutenant Colonel Ernest Swinton, a leading light in the tank's development.

The new armoured vehicles began arriving in Dorset in November 1917, transported by rail as far as Wool Station, then continuing by road to Bovington. The road was closed and those civilians living alongside were ordered to draw their blinds and sit in their back rooms until the tanks had trundled past. Anyone found walking along the route was made to turn their backs. All went well until some tanks apparently broke down in the middle of Bovington, putting paid to the efforts to keep them secret.

The tank's first significant success came in November 1917 during the Battle of Cambrai, when more than 400 vehicles penetrated almost 6 miles of a 7-mile front. They went on to play an important part in the offensives of 1918. Today, their modern counterparts can still be seen rolling across the hummocky Dorset grassland, just as their predecessors did 100 years ago, because Bovington is the headquarters of the Royal Armoured Corps and also the location of the renowned Tank Museum.

Another of Dorset's wartime secrets was the Royal Naval Cordite Factory at Holton Heath, a remote backwater of Poole Harbour, where explosive propellant was manufactured for the naval guns. It employed around 2,000 people, half of whom were women who travelled to work each day on trains which became known locally as 'glamour puffers'. The factory's production processes were so hazardous and vulnerable

The *Melcombe Regis*, one of Cosens' pre-war fleet of paddle-steamers, was used for coastal work during the conflict but survived intact.
(Courtesy of Weymouth Library, Ref: L.387.5.Cos.1).

to sabotage, that the site was surrounded by 12ft railings and guarded by a detachment of armed Metropolitan Police throughout the war.

The conflict's insatiable demand for munitions and other equipment was a boon for many businesses, but not all firms prospered. Cosens of Weymouth found it more of a struggle with each passing year to keep its business going now that priority was given to the war effort. With a history stretching back to 1848, the company had always relied on its famous paddle-steamers 'with buff funnels and black tops' to ply the south-west coast each summer, taking holiday makers on excursions. But the declaration of war quickly drew such passenger trade to a halt and Cosens now had to rely on other branches of its work, such as its tugs for rescue and salvage, and a busy engineering and ship-repairing business, to keep its head above water.

The year 1913 had been particularly successful for Cosens, with

Naval picket boats ferry 'liberty men' back to their ships. This is thought to be a wartime shot, taken in Weymouth backwater alongside the Cosens works. *(Courtesy of the Sandes family).*

directors praising the fine weather which had allowed a busy summer of steamboat excursions. The following year told a very different story, as the directors reported in their annual report to shareholders:

> 'In common with practically every other steamboat excursion company in England, the terrible war has materially interfered with our business ... Steamer traffic was interfered with to such an extent, that at one time it was under serious contemplation to lay all the vessels up.'

Worse was to come in 1915, when the Admiralty commandeered three paddle-steamers for war work (with more to follow), paying minimal compensation because the Government was keen to keep costs down. 'The returns from this service were very much less than the amount the board expected or considered due to them,' complained the directors.

The Admiralty also cancelled its contract with Cosens to ferry men and goods from ship to shore, because there were now so few naval ships in Portland or Weymouth Bay. This came as a blow because new vessels had just been bought for the purpose. 'We earnestly hope that not only in the interest of this company, but also of the town and neighbourhood, HM Ships will on the termination of the war, again make Portland harbour the chief place of assembly on the south coast,' the directors wrote.

In 1916 one of Cosens' much-loved paddle-steamers, the *Majestic*, was lost on active service in the Mediterranean. Converted into a minesweeper, she had been en route to Malta in a small convoy, heavily laden with coal, when she foundered, probably due to shipping water through a porthole. An eye-witness later recalled: 'One of the ports had not been fastened properly and the water got in. The pumps were clogged with small coal in the bilge and down she went.' Fortunately, the weather was calm and there were no casualties.

A photograph of the *Majestic* just before she went down would hang in the Cosens boardroom for many years.

By 1917 an acceptance of the war had crept into the annual report, giving it a more phlegmatic tone:

'The usual steamboat excursions made by the company's steamers have again been entirely abandoned, but the majority of vessels have been employed on war work for the Government and in addition, the engineering branch of the company's business has been almost entirely engaged on Work of National Importance.'

The following year a shortage of manpower proved a sticking point, but as the war drew to a close the Cosens directors allowed themselves a pat on the back for keeping the company going through four testing years:

'Much difficulty was experienced in obtaining the necessary labour and in consequence, the amount of work turned out was probably not so great as in earlier periods of the war,

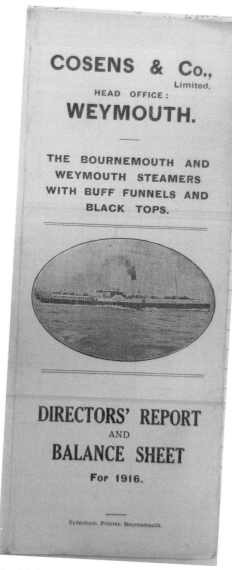

COSENS & Co., Limited,

HEAD OFFICE:

WEYMOUTH.

THE BOURNEMOUTH AND WEYMOUTH STEAMERS WITH BUFF FUNNELS AND BLACK TOPS.

DIRECTORS' REPORT

AND

BALANCE SHEET

For 1916.

Sydenham, Printer, Bournemouth.

The *Majestic*'s picture had always featured on the Cosens annual company report, but her name was removed after she foundered in 1916.

(Courtesy of Weymouth Library, Ref: L.387.5.Cos.1).

although your company has much to be congratulated on in actually keeping the works department going, owing to the demands made by the Government for men.'

A very different story emerged from the Whitehead Torpedo Works at Wyke Regis, then a village at the southern tip of Weymouth. The company had been operating since 1891 and was a major employer in the area, having built housing, such as the Ferrybridge Cottages for its workers and also paid for two local schools to be built.

Torpedoes were vital for the Royal Navy and were used by British submarines, as well as all types of surface vessels, to sink hostile German and Turkish vessels. Larger and faster torpedoes were designed at Whitehead's for the Royal Navy as a matter of urgency and thousands were turned out during the war. Production continued around the clock, with hundreds of workers alighting at the Wyke Regis rail halt each day.

Each torpedo was very expensive to produce and naval historian Stuart Morris has calculated that each one would have cost the equivalent of around £60,000-70,000. Powered by their own

Whitehead Torpedo Works in the early 1900s; ironically this postcard was produced by a German firm, as were many others at the time, and could well have proved useful to German wartime intelligence!
(Courtesy of the Eddie Prowse Collection).

24 THURSDAY [55—311]

S. Matthias.

Range. Took down enormous wire from greenock miles long, only 1 word wrong! Iey. got 1st pay! 15/10 for 4 days. Bought meringues & cream buns for supper! Nereids doing challenging

25 FRIDAY [56—310]

Rang. learned to time Torpedoes with stopwatch, in Observation Room. snowstorm, S. still in bed. Australians & wounded snowballed me.

'Took down enormous wire from Greenock miles long, only one word wrong!' wrote Madge Sneyd-Kynnersley in her diary. *(Courtesy of the Sandes Family).*

compressed-air engine and able to run a pre-set course once fired, they were a primitive form of guided missile.

The weapons were tested just around the corner from Whitehead's, at the Royal Navy's torpedo range at Bincleaves, in Portland Harbour. It was here that Madge Sneyd-Kynnersley, having tired of nursing, took a job as a clerk in 1916 and her diary gives an insight into the busy days at the Admiralty office. Her duties were split between wages and handling torpedo information, the latter being a challenge she obviously enjoyed: 'Took down enormous wire from Greenock [a Royal Naval Torpedo Factory in Scotland] miles long, only one word wrong!' she wrote in her diary.

Madge Sneyd-Kynnersley found her job at the torpedo range challenging and interesting at first, but as the workload increased her morale sank. *(Courtesy of the Sandes Family).*

A few days later: 'Code wire came from Gosport and we stayed till 6.45 trying to decode it. At last I was the one to find the clue.' When her boss was away one day she took the opportunity to have a good look around: 'I went all over shop and saw dynamos, gyros being tested, boilers and all parts of torpedoes. V interesting,' she wrote, adding, 'sardines on toast for lunch in big office.'

There were often light-hearted moments, as when racing tips appeared on the telegraph wire instead of the expected torpedo figures: 'Took code wire all about 'black dog' 'nicky nan' etc and discovered it was racing so rang up Dr Wetherall [a family friend] and put 10 shillings on Salandra (horse mentioned) which won 15/8 on.'

Madge relished the chance to learn new skills, such as semaphore and morse code. She was soon capable of firing torpedoes from a boat on the ranges, timing them with a stopwatch from the observation room, and recording the test data. 'Went on targets 600yd and 1500yd ones, had torpedoes fired under us, 'L' torpedo or a Mk V111. Did igniter turn on hektograph [a printer],' she noted.

Not all tests went according to plan and a number of torpedoes ended up careering around the harbour and beyond, with some vessels being hit in consequence. Armed only with dummy warheads, however, casualties were mercifully few. Madge records one incident during which a torpedo was fired through the harbour's defence boom, and on more than one occasion porpoises got in the way of testing: 'Mr Prior fired a torpedo at them but they didn't mind.' Madge enjoyed a ringside seat when drama occurred at sea: 'Three ships torpedoed near here this weekend so all office staff went out and inspected an 8,000-ton steamer near Whitehead's and poked pole in hole. Very foggy ... later we went out in fog to seek P&O [another damaged ship] but it hadn't come in.'

However, as the months passed and her workload increased, Madge's morale dwindled as more and more was asked of the staff. Lunch had been cut to half an hour, bank holidays had been abolished ('as munitions must not be delayed') and in March 1917 an order came through for staff to work until 4pm on Saturdays. Madge fired off a 'killing' letter to her boss, complaining that the demands being made were 'not conducive to self respect' and were a 'retarding influence of lack of appreciation and encouragement'. But her protest came to nothing.

A few days later, yet another order was issued requesting that two out of three staff should be on duty every Sunday morning, and at the end of November a new cause for concern had cropped up: 'Fearful worries as Greenock and Ad [Admiralty] want us to pass 40 new torps a week instead of 10 and air compressors can't pump air quickly enough.'

For many women, going to work was nothing new. By the beginning of last century, a large proportion of working class women and girls were spending long hours in factories and as domestic servants in order to make ends meet. In contrast, entering the workplace was a revolutionary step for women among the upper and middle classes, like Madge, especially because they were taking over from men. Many took on white collar jobs in offices, government departments and shops, which had previously been the preserve of men.

Women also made up a large proportion of the wartime workforce in factories and industry, where heavy and hazardous work was often demanded of them. At gas works, for example, they stoked furnaces; at shipyards they operated cranes and winches; and at shell-filling factories they risked their health – and sometimes their lives – preparing weapons for the Front.

A recruiting poster for the Women's Land Army, established in 1917 to address the shortage of farm labour.
(Courtesy of the Library of Congress, Reproduction Number LC-USZC4-11192).

There was no large-scale manufacture of munitions in Weymouth, Dorchester or Portland, although small firms adapted their production to help the war effort wherever possible. Companies like Channons of Dorchester, which had built and sold motorcars before the war, now made parts for gun carriages and by 1918 its workforce was almost exclusively female.

During the course of the war, thousands of women nationwide worked in agriculture, many under the auspices of the Women's Land Army, which was formally established in 1917 to address the shortage of farm labour and also the need for more food to be grown at home. The scheme was a great success in Dorset, although initially many farmers had been prejudiced, believing either that women were not up to the job, or that it would be ungentlemanly to recruit them for hard manual labour. Training centres were set up, women-only billets provided accommodation where necessary, and in May 1917 the county organiser, the Hon Mrs Eleanor Grant, wrote to the *Western Gazette*:

'The keenness of the women to learn, inspired by the patriotic motives which have brought them out on to the land, go far to supplement the deficiencies of technical and muscular skill, which time alone can make good.'

By January 1918, 1,100 women were employed on Dorset farms and the chairman of the county's War Agricultural Committee, Mr G. H. Gordon, was proud to report that, whereas several counties had 'turned their back' on female labour, 'Dorset was not one of them'.

The chance to work was welcomed by married women, forced to find jobs after the deaths of their husbands, and by single women like the Sneyd-Kynnersleys, who would otherwise have obeyed social convention and remained at home until they found suitable spouses. In the years leading up to the conflict, the sisters' days had been spent in a round of leisure activities: bathing, playing tennis, calling on friends, and enjoying band concerts in summer, while winter was devoted to badminton and bridge, roller-skating, and shopping. It sounds like a charmed existence but there was little to challenge, stimulate or satisfy such intelligent and well-educated young women. 'My mother said she wondered sometimes what she would do with her days because there was no career,' recalled Sylvia's daughter, Penelope, many years later.

All four sisters volunteered as Red Cross nurses when hostilities began, but the role did not really suit Sylvia and Madge, especially when they had to take orders from professional nurses who sometimes looked down their noses at untrained volunteers. The following incident was reported in Madge's diary:

'Miss Millar had day off and me the only Red Cross nurse in ward. So very hard work. I quarrelled with horrible Sister Reny who slanged me for not getting No 19 his milk and said I must learn to do as she told me. I said well sister I can't make milk can I, she replied I didn't ask you to make milk or milk a cow and if I have any more impertinence I will report you to your commandant!'

It wasn't long before Madge and Sylvia had registered at the local labour exchange for alternative work. Among the jobs in which they expressed interest were chauffeuring, dairy work and poultry farming. In the end, both became clerks – Madge at Bincleaves, as previously mentioned, and Sylvia in a variety of offices, where she observed life with an ironic eye. Her first clerking role was with the Exeter Army Pay Office, a job she hadn't really wanted:

'I was given an appointment for an interview, but on arrival at the office I conceived so great a dislike for it that I determined to fail my "test". This proved to consist of sums in simple arithmetic, and

Sylvia Sneyd Kynnersley's ironic take on office life at Dorchester Recruiting Office, where she worked as a clerk in 1917.
(Courtesy of the Sandes family).

having done them hopelessly wrong, I cheerfully handed in my paper, saying I feared I had not the necessary gifts. To my dismay I was told it did not matter, as I was obviously the "right sort of girl". So I was enrolled as a Clerk (female) at 19 shillings a week.

'In this office I spent several months, the first three weeks of each passed in complete idleness, and the fourth in a hectic rush of Pay and Mess Books.'

Her next position was at Dorchester Recruiting Office and here she put her talent for drawing to good use, with a sketch based on Lord Kitchener's 'Your country needs YOU' posters. At the top, in bold red, were the words 'Are YOU in this?' Below, one woman sits at her desk working, another snoozes with her head on her arms and a third tucks into a box of chocolates.

Kitty and Rosie Sneyd-Kynnersley, on the other hand, remained working as Red Cross nurses. Kitty, the oldest, worked first in Weymouth, then at University Hospital in London, and was later posted to hospitals in other parts of the country. Her aim had been to serve in France, but this wasn't to be. Her disappointment was recorded by her sister Madge: 'Met Susan [a family friend] who said she had notice to be ready to start for France in 24hrs. Poor K only told she is placed on

Kitty Sneyd-Kynnersley worked as a Red Cross nurse in Weymouth and elsewhere in Britain during the war, but was disappointed not to be posted abroad. *(Courtesy of the Sandes family).*

Rosie Sneyd-Kynnersley volunteered as a nurse when war broke out, and by 1918 had become the commandant of a Red Cross hospital in Weymouth. *(Courtesy of the Sandes family).*

Reserve List of nurses and need not be prepared yet. Very galling.'

Rosie, the youngest Sneyd-Kynnersley sister, began the war as a volunteer nurse and climbed the ranks to become commandant of a Red Cross hospital in Weymouth, probably the Ryme Hospital which overlooked Portland Harbour from Old Castle Road. She documented her wartime work by taking snapshots of hospital life and these images show how relaxed men and women, who may once have stood on ceremony, now were in each other's company. After the war, Rosie continued her work with the Red Cross and, at the end of the Second World War, spent a year in Germany working as a chaplain's assistant with the British Army of the Rhine. During this time she witnessed proceedings at the Belsen war crimes trial at Lüneberg.

Her sister Madge went on to have two novels published, one of which

(Above, below and overleaf) At ease: Rosie Sneyd-Kynnersley's relaxed shots of soldiers and nurses at Princess Christian Hospital, Weymouth, in 1917. *(Courtesy of the Sandes family).*

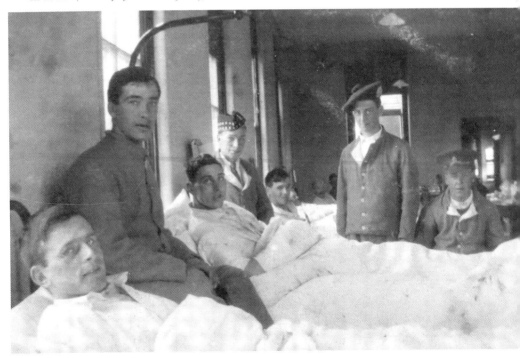

was a humorous romance entitled *Smoke Without Fire*. Set in the East Indies, it was widely reviewed when it came out in 1934, with the author described as 'wittily sarcastic' and 'engagingly spiteful'. Sylvia Sneyd-Kynnersley became a frequent contributor of articles to magazines and newspapers, while Kitty settled down in Weymouth where she took a particular interest in the welfare of animals.

The war gave British women the opportunity to take up positions of responsibility, but many men stood firm in their old Edwardian attitudes and refused to accept women as their equals. This was illustrated when Dorothy Baker was put forward for the job of 'head

The war provided job opportunities for women like this pharmacist at Princess Christian Hospital, Weymouth. *(Courtesy of the Sandes family).*

postman' at Dorchester Post Office in 1916. The original head postman had left to go and fight, as had his replacement, and with a decreasing number of men left to choose from, the district postmaster, Walter Drew, considered Mrs Baker by far the best candidate. She had joined the Post Office the previous year and he had been impressed by her organisational skills and confidence, both of which would be useful in a job that involved supervising postmen, checking overweight packages,

Queen Alexandra was the patroness of the Field Force Fund, founded in October 1914 to provide 'comforts' for troops during the First World War.
(Courtesy of Taylor Library).

examining bicycles, and handling enquiries from the public.

However, when Mr Drew recommended Mrs Baker his superiors were not enthusiastic. They approved her appointment 'as an experiment' only and decided not to pay her the full 5 shillings extra allowance that the head postmen usually received each week. When objections were raised they remained unconvinced: 'Mr Drew, will you be so good as to say whether Mrs Baker performs the whole of the head postman's duties?' they asked doubtfully. 'Mrs Baker performs the whole of the head postman's duties,' was his curt reply.

Mrs Baker stood her ground, but only after a long struggle did the Post Office bosses finally agree to pay her the allowance her male predecessors had received without question.

Women's contribution to the war effort cannot be overestimated, not only among those who performed paid work but also the volunteers who gave their time. They bolstered morale by organizing concerts, visited and helped entertain the wounded in hospital, and raised money for good causes. Flag-selling on the streets became popular and money raised went towards everything from the Red Cross and Russian relief to helping wounded horses.

On Portland, the Easton Ladies' Sewing Guild worked tirelessly throughout the war to make warm clothing and 'comforts' for servicemen. The Guild kept a neat record book, logging details of the articles each member had made and where they were sent. Servicemen based locally were the first to benefit, with the following garments delivered to Breakwater Fort on 10 September 1914:

17 shirts

5 helmets [balaclavas]

6 comforters [knitted caps]

40 bags

12 pairs socks

In October, more items were sent to Blacknor Fort on the west of Portland, and in November it was the turn of troops at the Verne Citadel to receive their share of socks and comforters.

The ladies of Easton rallied to the call of national organisations like Queen Alexandra's Field Force Fund, which aimed to 'promote the well-being of the Expeditionary Forces'. At the helm of this body were the great and the good of wartime Britain: Her Majesty the Queen was patroness; the president was Viscountess French, wife of General Sir John French who commanded the British Expeditionary Force in Europe during the first months of war; and it was chaired by Countess of Bective, a woman often described as 'redoubtable'.

From its Knightsbridge headquarters, the Fund sent out letters appealing for support to local groups like the Easton Ladies' Sewing Guild:

'The committee of the fund feel it their duty to make adequate

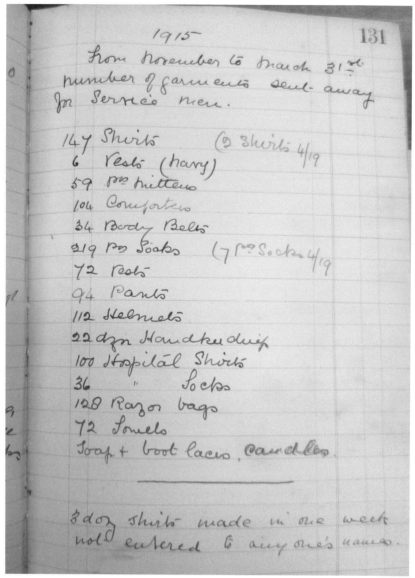

1915   131

From November to march 31st number of garments sent away for Service men.

147 Shirts   (2 Shirts 4/19
6 Vests (navy)
59 pr mittens
104 Comforters
34 Body Belts
219 pr Socks   (7 pr Socks 4/19
72 pots
94 Pants
112 Helmets
22 dzn Handkerchief
100 Hospital Shirts
36 "   Socks
128 Razor bags
72 Towels
Soap + boot laces, Candles.

_____

3 doz shirts made in one week not entered to any one's names.

A page from the meticulously kept wartime records of the Easton Ladies' Sewing Guild. *(Courtesy of Portland Heritage Trust).*

provision in good time for the probable needs of the Overseas Forces during the coming winter. They accordingly renew their appeal to you to again help them during the next months, as you have so generously and continuously done in the past, by making or collecting such articles of warm clothing as mufflers, socks, mittens, woollen helmets, underclothing and sweaters.'

The ladies of Easton dutifully pasted the letter into their record book and set to work, producing in one five-month period: 147 shirts, 72 vests, 92 pants and 112 helmets, 22 dozen handkerchiefs, 100 hospital shirts, 128 razor bags, 72 towels 59 pairs of mittens, 104 comforters, and 219 pairs of socks.

Garments supplied to servicemen by the public weren't always particularly comfortable. Shirts were often rough, and one famous wartime song gently mocked the work of one young seamstress:

'Sister Susie's sewing shirts for soldiers
Such skill at sewing shirts our shy young sister Susie shows!
Some soldiers send epistles, say they'd sooner sleep in thistles
Than the saucy, soft, short shirts for soldiers sister Susie sews.

'Piles and piles and piles of shirts she sends out to the soldiers,
And sailors won't be jealous when they see them, not at all.
And when we say her stitching will set all the soldiers itching,
She says our soldiers fight best when their backs are 'gainst the wall.'

Wool could be coarse too, especially when worn next to the skin, but the freezing and miserable conditions in the trenches meant that anything offering a bit of extra warmth was welcome, especially socks which were frequently requested in letters home. Even better, hand-made garments showed that someone at home was thinking of them.

Knitting caught on quickly when war was declared, it was an easy way for civilians to contribute and a skill that many already had. Women, men and children began making their own 'comforts' for the troops and the clicking of needles could often be heard in public places. At one railway station it was reported that a lady waiting for her train knitted the first few inches of a muffler (as scarves were then known), then left the knitting with a note encouraging the next waiting passenger to take it up.

Women's magazines were full of knitting-

A wartime booklet produced by Weldon's, a publisher of paper patterns, with instructions on how to make 'Garments and hospital comforts for our soldiers and sailors'. Items included knitted socks and a sleeping helmet. *(Author's collection)*.

related advice, patterns, and advertisements. One yarn merchant sang the praises of his wool, which came in navy blue for sailors and khaki for soldiers and, he claimed, was well-suited to the demands of life at the Front:

> 'My wool is manufactured from Long Staple yarn, and has been thoroughly shrunk, so that all danger of the garment shrinking is diminished … We guarantee quality, and can supply the finest wool, specially prepared for knitting Socks, Mufflers, Helmets &c for Army and Navy wear.'

Back on Portland, the Easton Ladies Sewing Guild also made clothing for Belgian refugees, and destitute women and children in Serbia. These more delicate garments bound for eastern Europe made poignant reading, with babies' blankets, bloomers, petticoats, chemises and dresses listed, among more workaday items like shirts, socks and mufflers.

In November 1917 a big fair was held on Portland to raise money for Serbian civilians, whose wretched lives were described on a poster advertising the event at Jubilee Hall in Easton Square. Under the heading 'Portland's effort for starving Serbia', it read:

'Austro-Hungarians, Germans and Bulgarians have taken and carried away the whole of this year's harvest, which was very abundant. The unfortunate inhabitants are being deprived of all kinds of foodstuffs. There is practically no milk in Serbia, and the children are dying by thousands.'

People were asked to donate old furniture, clothes, antiques, books, music, china, 'perambulators', even coal. A collection depot was set up in the hamlet of Wakeham, and a

A poster advertising 'Portland's effort for starving Serbia', an event held in November 1917.

(Courtesy of Portland Heritage Trust).

Officers and NCOs of Weymouth's Volunteer Training Battalion 1914-19.
(Courtesy of Weymouth Library, Ref: L779.99403 JAR.1).

collection service was offered for those who couldn't struggle that far with their goods.

Civilian men too were willing to give their time for the war effort. Those who were unable to serve set up their own volunteer battalions in South Dorset and across the country, to help enforce security at home, rather like the Home Guard in the Second World War. Most of the men in question were either too old to serve, or were prevented from doing so because they worked in jobs deemed of national importance.

These Volunteer Training Battalions were often led by retired army officers, but early in the war they faced frustration because the War Office refused to give the units official recognition. As a result they had to be self-funding, provide their own uniforms – which could *not* be khaki – and wear distinguishing armbands, with the letters G. R., for Georgius Rex (Latin for 'King George'). This led to inevitable mockery from some members of the public, who joked that the initials stood for

'George's Wrecks', 'Grandpa's Regiment' or 'Government Rejects'.

It wasn't until 1916 that the War Office finally took the volunteers seriously and included their battalions in the county infantry regiment system. Thereafter they were put to good use, performing tasks ranging from guarding vulnerable sites and handling munitions to helping with the harvest, fire-fighting and transporting wounded soldiers. In 1917 members began to be issued with rifles and machine guns, and by 1918 the volunteer battalions counted 285,000 among their ranks nationally.

The fight for recognition left some feeling disillusioned and this is perhaps evident at the end of a letter of thanks written by Lieutenant Edwards, commanding officer of the Portland volunteer detachment, to the Easton Ladies Sewing Guild for items they had provided: 'On behalf of my detachment may I very sincerely thank you and the Ladies of the Easton Guild for their prompt and kind gift ... If everything in connection with the war was done with the same thoroughness it would soon be over.'

***

It would be wrong to suggest that the war brought out the best in everyone. The list of criminal cases heard in the Assize Court at Shire Hall, Dorchester throughout 1917, tells a very different story. Plenty of servicemen appeared on charges often related to forgery, fraud, bigamy and rape. Women were also among the accused, but their crimes were generally more suggestive of tangled and unhappy lives. In 1917 the following women were among those tried at Dorchester; for them, the war was probably no more than a backdrop to their own misery:

> January – A domestic servant murders her baby girl and confesses to concealment of the birth.

> May – A 41-year-old woman attempts 'to kill and murder herself' (at this time suicide was regarded as a crime).

> October – A 32-year-old woman confesses to using an instrument to procure a miscarriage for another woman.

In homes everywhere, families were learning to live with the fear that bad news could arrive at any time, and when it did, comfort was often found in sending a few brief lines to the local newspaper. The following item appeared in the *Western Gazette* on 30 November 1917:

> 'IN HOSPITAL. – Mr and Mrs Cumbleton, of Poundbury, have received information from the War Office that their youngest son, Percy Cumbleton has been admitted to hospital in Egypt suffering

from gunshot wound in the right arm. This is the second son that has been wounded, and the third (and eldest) son, a sergeant-major, is still serving in France.'

Newspapers relied on readers to keep them informed, and this report was probably supplied by Mrs Cumbleton herself. During the course of the war the *Gazette* published several snippets about her three sons' military endeavours, in addition to those of her two brothers. Readers would have been alarmed to hear about Percy's plight, especially when worse followed next month: 'DANGEOUSLY ILL. – Mr and Mrs Cumbleton, of Poundbury, have been notified by the War Office that their youngest son, Percy Cumbleton has been admitted to Kantara Hospital having been wounded in action. His right arm and right leg have both been amputated.'

All went quiet for several weeks as Percy, a soldier with the 4th Dorsets, fought for his life. Then, in January 1918, came a more heartening announcement: 'Mrs and Mrs Cumbleton have received news that their son Percy ... has been brought safely to Bath War Hospital [in Somerset].'

The Gazette made no further mention of Percy, but in 1919 a short report appeared to say that the family's eldest son, Sergeant Major H. G. Cumbleton, had been awarded the Military Medal for bravery and devotion to duty.

Thoughts of you and Home.

Many a tear was shed by wives over loving postcards sent home from the Front by their husbands.

(Courtesy of David and Lorraine Judge).

The war was a trying time for mothers with young families, as well as those with sons at the Front. To them alone fell the task of comforting youngsters who were missing their fathers, coping with the family budget – a new responsibility for most – and making sure there was enough food on the table when even potatoes could be hard to find. When the children had gone to bed, letters from the Front would be pulled out and re-read, and tears shed over loving postcards that had been hurriedly sent.

Some young women had yet to find husbands and, with casualty lists growing by the day, they may already have been anticipating a life of spinsterhood when the war was over. Among these young women may have been 'Annie', who wrote this verse in her friend Maggie Watson's autograph book one evening in April 1917, as they shared a drink at the Crown Hotel in Weymouth:

'I wish I had someone to love me,
And someone to see me straight home,
And someone to go to bed with me,
For I am tired of sleeping alone.'

***

When war broke out, Britain depended on overseas imports for around 60 per cent of her food, which made the country vulnerable to any disruption in the supply. Well aware of this weakness, Germany began targeting merchant ships with its U-boats in an attempt to starve Britain into submission. As a result large numbers of ships and the goods they were carrying were lost. In April 1917 alone an unprecedented 550,000 tons of shipping was sunk. The effects were felt at home through food shortages, rising prices, and long queues outside shops. The anti-social practices of hoarding by those wealthy enough to lay in stocks, and profiteering made the situation even worse.

The public were asked to shop sensibly, to think of others, and somehow the country struggled on. But in the end there was no option but to introduce rationing. Sugar was the first commodity to be controlled in this way. Before the war, most of Britain's sugar had come from beet grown in Germany and Austria, now it came from cane grown in Britain's colonies. In July 1917, householders were issued with ration cards which entitled them to half a pound of sugar each week, and in 1918 rationing would be extended to other foods like meat, butter, cheese and margarine.

Despite rationing, people were allowed to apply for extra quantities of sugar in order to make jam from fruit they had grown themselves. In Portland there was a mild scandal when schoolmaster William Edwards, who was also a magistrate and local councillor, was accused of acting 'in a spirit of selfishness' in obtaining 1cwt of sugar (almost 51kgs) for this purpose. The police court was told that he had a large garden full of fruit, and while it was agreed that he hadn't breached any rules, 'it was in no means by good taste that Mr Edwards, occupying as he did a position of importance ... had obtained sugar in the quantity he had, when other people couldn't get it for neither love nor money.'

Householders were encouraged to grow their own food and – ever a nation of gardeners – they were very receptive to the idea. Flower beds and lawns were turned into vegetable patches, many began to keep poultry in their back gardens, and the Government commandeered large areas of idle land for use as allotments.

Gardening inspired a generous spirit, for example a column called 'The Garden' in the *Western Gazette*, was headed by this earnest message: 'If any reader who is in difficulty with reference to his garden will write directly to the address given beneath, his questions will all be answered, free of charge, in full detail, and by return of post – Ed.' Then it was on to the business of the day: 'Notes on manures (continued from last week).'

Village institutes also did their best to provide help and advice and at the end of one fruit-bottling demonstration at Upwey it was announced that 'Mr Ismay would willingly lend the apparatus used to anyone wishing to make use of it for fruit preserving.'

The range of comestibles grown in gardens and allotments was impressive, as can be seen from these hints passed on to readers by the *Western Gazette*'s by 'Spade-Worker' in his December column:

'Seed potatoes: My experience is that it does not pay to continue to plant home grown "seed".

'Storing root crops: One may leave beetroot, carrot, parsnip, turnip, salsafy [sic] and scorzonera [both root crops with a taste reminiscent of oysters] in the ground and dig them up as required.

'Pruning apples and pears: The leading shoots at the end of the branches ought now to be shortened by one third, or one half if weak.'

***

The year finished on a depressing note for Weymouth, when one of the most destructive fires the town had seen in years ripped through Templeman's Flour Mills on the Quay. Not only was the main building gutted but large quantities of much-needed wheat and cereals were lost too. While the fire brigade struggled to extinguish the blaze, Australian troops based in the town restrained the crowd of onlookers. Meanwhile, nearby residents were seen desperately throwing their belongings out of windows; at one property a piano was even lowered down.

When the blaze was extinguished there were mumblings that more could have been done to save the mill, but with most local young men now at the Front, the fire brigade was in a difficult position. 'The Captain of the Fire Brigade laments the fact that he is only left with a staff advanced in years, many of whom are only waiting until the end of the war to retire,' reported the local press. No cause for the fire was given.

If things were gloomy in Britain they were verging on catastrophic in Germany, where the Allied blockade was biting far more deeply than the German U-boat campaign. This is how one newspaper correspondent in Basle described the plight of German civilians at the end of 1917:

'The most striking feature of the German Christmas was the great and plainly evident misery of the people. All day long ill-clad women and children were openly begging food in the snow covered streets, and in many cases making daring attempts to steal what they could not obtain by charity. Hunger riots are reported from several towns, the most serious of the disturbances being in Cologne, where the price of all ordinary necessaries has soared to heights far beyond the resources of the people ... Most of the churches have been closed owing to the lack of fuel for heating purposes ... Only a miracle can prevent the death by starvation of thousands of people.'

In comparison, the people of Dorset still had a lot to be thankful for.

Chapter Five

1918 – A CHANGED WORLD

WINTRY WEATHER BROUGHT gales, snow and rough seas to southern England during the first weeks of 1918 and, after three years of conflict, most people saw little reason to be optimistic when they rang in the New Year. With no sign of an end to the fighting, Britons had settled down to lives in which hardships predominated and bad news from the Front could arrive at any moment. Few could have predicted that this was the year the Great War would end.

Lack of goods in the shops made life trying, as Madge Sneyd-Kynnersley noted in her diary on 19 January – 'Shortage of meat', and on 2 February – 'No marg or butter for 2 days'. This also gave unscrupulous traders an opportunity for profiteering and in Dorchester these practices were observed with an eagle eye by none other than Thomas Hardy, the Dorset novelist. After the war, Hardy spoke about wartime life in the area with fellow writer Robert Graves who, in turn, recorded their conversation in his book *Goodbye to All That*:

> 'He [Hardy] described his war-work, rejoicing to have been chairman of the Anti-Profiteering Committee, and to have succeeded in bringing a number of rascally Dorchester tradesmen to book. "It made me unpopular, of course," he admitted, "but it was a hundred times better than sitting on a Military Tribunal and sending young men to the war who did not want to go."

Local newspapers carried detailed reports of cases like that of grocer Charles Smith, who ran the County Stores in Dorchester High East Street. Maximum prices for some foods were now being set by the Government and Smith was discovered to have sold ground rice at 5d per lb, instead of the revised price of 4½d. He told magistrates that, even though he was a member of Dorchester's Food Control Committee, he hadn't been aware of the change and this was

Dorchester novelist Thomas Hardy kept an eye on unscrupulous traders during the war.

merely an inadvertent mistake. The magistrates were in no mood to be lenient and fined him £15, dismissing his excuse as 'absolutely ridiculous'.

Mr Smith's case would have resonated with other shopkeepers because it wasn't always easy to keep up with the complicated and ever-changing schedule of 'official' prices. Many protested that they thought their price had been correct, but more often than not courts preferred to take the side of the public.

Defendants like Annie Pomeroy, the manageress of the International Stores in South Street, Dorchester, must have felt very hard done by. She received a conviction and a £3 fine after being accused of charging 1s 1d for a packet of Sylvan Glen oats, when the price should have been 11d. Miss Pomeroy explained that her price had been sent down by head office in London and that she had simply been 'obeying orders'. Magistrates considered that, as manageress of the branch, she was responsible for the conduct of the business.

It wasn't just shopkeepers who were prosecuted for transgressing the new rules. Sidney Roberts of Salisbury Street, Fordington, was summonsed to appear before magistrates as a warning to others who were purchasing meat from non-registered retailers, paying cash instead of their ration coupons. Roberts was one of many who had been buying rabbits in this way from Dorchester market. This was manifestly unfair, as it enabled people to use their coupons to purchase meat elsewhere, said the chairman of the magistrates. Roberts was fined 5 shillings.

Domestic life was now dominated by a plethora of rules and regulations, but however annoying they could be to the general public, they would soon be rendered insignificant by an event of far greater consequence: the launch of a German offensive that would eventually lead to an end to the conflict. Known as the 'Kaiserschlacht', it drew on troops who had been released from the Eastern Front following the collapse of Russia. The aim was to overwhelm Allied forces in a series of attacks along the Western Front, principally in sectors held by the British Army, before American troops, who had joined the conflict in 1917, could arrive in large numbers.

When the offensive began on 21 March it took everyone by surprise and struck fear into Margaret Sneyd-Kynnersley, who had just begun the annual spring-clean of her Weymouth home. 'The great offensive began,' she wrote with alarm. 'Terrible fighting.' During those early weeks, Mrs Sneyd-Kynnersley's diary reflected the uncertain future Britain faced as the Germans advanced with speed, leaving chaos in their wake.

To a woman born in 1884, who had grown up during an era when the might of Britain and her Empire had never been questioned, this was a cause of great concern:

> 31 March (Easter Day) – 'A day of great gloom and anxiety. I never before knew such a terrible fear for our country.'

> 6 April – 'Awful battles raging round Amiens – great anxiety.'

> 7 April – 'Very great anxiety, Amiens not yet taken.'

> 9 April – 'Terrible fighting.'

> 11 April – 'I had 3 wounded [from a local hospital] to tea, one from the new offensive.'

Margaret Sneyd-Kynnersley came from a wealthy Northumberland family and had moved south with her four daughters after the death of her husband, a successful civil engineer. Her outlook on life was Edwardian, rooted in a social structure in which everyone knew their place, and she struggled to come to terms not only with Britain's new vulnerability, but other changes that the war had wrought at home, particularly the increasing difficulty of finding domestic servants.

Margaret Sneyd-Kynnersley was concerned not only about the country's future, but also the shortage of domestic staff during the spring of 1918.
(Courtesy of the Sandes family).

Before the war, large numbers of working class women had been employed in domestic service. Now, with new opportunities in the workplace and jobs offering them better pay, they were no longer reliant upon employers like Mrs Sneyd-Kynnersley, as this sequence of entries from her diary in September 1918, shows:

> 'Gladys Meyes [maid] came.'

> 'Dorothy most impertinent, I gave her a month's notice.'

> 'Mrs Bush came, a temporary cook but she was horrid.'

> 'Gladys left, sent off Mrs Bush.'

> 'Dorothy behaved so badly I set her away too – no maids.'

Margaret's daughter Sylvia helped out as best she could around the house and appears to have risen to the challenge:

> 'Up and got breakfast. Then housework, and washing up and cooking. Mother made lovely omelette.'

'Washing and household work. We make omelette and all sorts of things and get on beautifully.'

'Went to Dorchester and got maid's address and interviewed her but in the end came to nothing!'

'Chops for lunch, fairly easy.'

Then, at last, came some good news: 'Mrs Samway, my find, came to char and seems very nice and an excellent worker – a great relief for us not to have to do the sweeping and clean kitchen!'

Also turning Britain's old social structure on its head was the military. As those in charge desperately sought to keep the Front supplied with good soldiers, young and able men from lower down the social scale were now being promoted over the heads of their one-time civilian bosses. The result was illustrated in a rather gleeful sketch in an autograph book signed by servicemen convalescing in Weymouth. Entitled 'War's Transmutations', it shows a once overbearing manager having to take orders from his former cowering clerk.

Above all, the conflict brought about enormous changes in the manner war was waged. One of the most impressive advances was in aeronautics, which was still in its infancy in 1914. At first aircraft were used simply for battlefield reconnaissance, but in a few short years they were transformed into machines capable of engaging in aerial combat and flying long distances to drop bombs. The army and navy initially operated separate air wings (the Royal Flying Corps and Royal Naval Air Service respectively) until they were merged into the new Royal Air Force in 1918.

The rigid Edwardian social structure was being transformed, as illustrated by this cartoon, 'War's Transmutations', penned by a soldier in a wartime autograph book.
(Courtesy of Weymouth Museum, Ref: LH/WA/020).

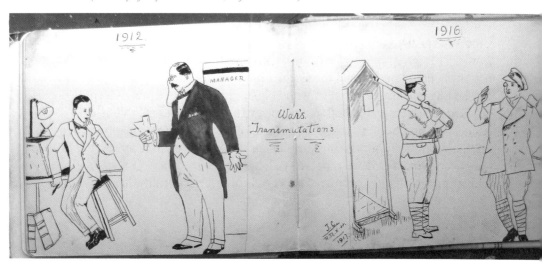

In 1916 breathtaking sights over a flying field at Chickerell, on the edge of Weymouth, caught the eye of Australian soldiers based at the nearby Westham and Monte Video army camps. One of them, Fred Martin, described what he saw in a letter to his father in July 1916:

'Had a game of cricket yesterday, Australians against Tommies, we had an easy win. There are tons of aircraft flying around here now that the summer is on. I am getting quite used to them. The latest invention holds four, five counting the driver. Two in charge of a machine gun in front and two in charge of a machine gun in the rear and the plane can do 120 miles an hour quite easily. The other day I saw a chap looping the loop. It was a grand sight.'

Sharp-eyed observers would also have spotted planes at Portland. These were the Admiralty's seaplanes or 'flying boats', which took off and landed on water using large floats in place of wheels. They were based at HMS *Sarepta*, also known as the Royal Naval Air Station Portland, which was established next to the existing naval base in 1916. The seaplanes were intended to patrol the coast off Portland for enemy submarines, which were active in the English Channel.

Sophisticated as seaplanes were, however, they relied on a fairly basic system of communications according to William Swailes, who was a boy on Portland during the Great War:

'The seaplanes were loaded with a bomb and went out looking for submarines. To help with communications between the aircraft and Portland a pigeon loft was built, a big one in the RN Hospital grounds. Each plane, when it was going off on patrol, took two or three of these pigeons in case they ditched! After the war the pigeon loft was taken down. Four of the pigeons were given to my father and we children had these four birds which eventually became 20 or more.'

Portland's Royal Naval Air Station set up a small satellite base at the Chickerell airfield in 1918, from which anti-submarine patrols were also flown. The aerodrome survived as an RAF station into the 1950s and now lies under housing and the Granby Industrial Estate.

The English Channel bristled with U-boats throughout the war, which targeted Allied shipping, both merchant and naval, without mercy. As a result, Portland became an important anti-submarine base. Converted trawlers were sent out to hunt the submarines, and minesweepers and destroyers were based there, possibly alongside the so-called 'Q Ships', which resembled ordinary merchant vessels but were, in reality, heavily

A seaplane, with floats visible instead of wheels, comes in to land at Portland Harbour, probably before the war. Whitehead's Torpedo Works is in the foreground. *(Courtesy of the Eddie Prowse Collection).*

Sir Douglas Haig greets troops at the Front: 'Every position must be held to the last man,' he urged British forces on 11 April 1918. *(Courtesy of Taylor Library).*

armed with concealed weapons. Their innocuous appearance was designed to decoy U-boats to the surface, so that they could be sunk more easily.

HMS *Sarepta* was also the base for an underwater-warfare research centre, which was developing listening devices to pick up the sound of U-boats. These early hydrophone systems were not the success the Admiralty had hoped for, but the research centre was later involved in pioneering work leading to the introduction of Sonar ahead of the Second World War.

On the wharves and jetties at Portland scenes of great industry could be observed during the war, with ships and men constantly coming and going. Young William Swailes watched from the waterside with fascination. 'I used to go all round the dockyard,' he recalled. 'I used to go to the coal heaps and watch the ships disgorging coal. Watch troopers coming in bringing troops from Australia and New Zealand in long lines. Saw the Japanese destroyers arrived – Japan was our ally in that war. I went aboard one of them and a sailor gave me a Japanese postcard.'

Portland was a major naval base, although not on the scale of Portsmouth, Devonport, Chatham or Rosyth. It did not have extensive naval barracks, nor dry docks in which ships could be refitted. But before the war, as a large protected harbour, it was used for training and for the assembly of the Fleet for exercises and Reviews, such as the concentration of the Grand Fleet in July 1914.

During the conflict Britain's warships were based in the North Sea, but occasional visits further south caused huge excitement in Weymouth. 'What a surprise,' wrote Madge Sneyd-Kynnersley in June 1916. 'Seven huge battleships (King Edwards) and several destroyers and a cruiser came in!!! Anchored in Roads, the first ships since autumn of 1914.' That evening – and any other occasion when big ships were in harbour – the town was full of sailors who came ashore to enjoy the nightlife.

In April 1918, however, Dorset eyes were firmly fixed on the Western Front. The German offensive was continuing and on 11 April Sir Douglas Haig, Commander-in-Chief of the British Armies in France, issued his famous 'Backs to the wall' communiqué to troops:

'Many amongst us now are tired. To those I would say that Victory will belong to the side which holds out the longest ... There is no other course open to us but to fight it out. Every position must be held to the last man: there must be no retirement. With our backs to the wall and believing in the justice of our cause each one of us must fight on to the end. The safety of our homes and the Freedom of mankind alike depend upon the conduct of each one of us at this critical moment.'

As the Allies fought back, the German Army began suffering heavy casualties and found it difficult to hold the ground it now occupied. 'News splendid – Germans driven back across the Marne,' wrote Margaret Sneyd-Kynnersley in July, her spirits revived. In August an Allied counter-offensive was launched which would drive the Germans back and force their eventual defeat, with the signing of an armistice that came into effect on 11 November 1918.

***

After more than four long years, the war that people had once assumed would be 'over by Christmas 1914' had finally drawn to a close. On 12 November newspapers trumpeted the Allied victory in bold, succinct

Newspaper headlines telling of the Armistice on 11 November 1918 prompted scenes of celebration all over South Dorset.
(Courtesy of Bristol Reference Library).

GERMANY'S HUMILIATION.

EVACUATION TO THE RHINE.

ALLIES TO OCCUPY BRIDGEHEADS.

ALL U-BOATS TO SURRENDER.

WARSHIPS TO DISARM: 5,000 GUNS FOR ALLIES.

RIGHT TO OCCUPY HELIGOLAND.

REPATRIATION WITHOUT RECIPROCITY

The great world war came to an end yesterday at 11 a.m. Yesterday was the 100th day of the fifth year. The following historic announcement was issued by Mr. Lloyd George at 10.20 yesterday morning.

THE ARMISTICE WAS SIGNED AT 5 a.m. THIS MORNING, AND HOSTILITIES ARE TO CEASE ON ALL FRONTS AT 11 a.m. TO-DAY.

Immediately following the signing of the armistice the following message was sent out by wireless:—

Marshal Foch to Commanders-in-Chief.

Hostilities will cease on the whole front as from November 11th at 11 o'clock (French time).

The Allied troops will not, until a further order, go beyond the line reached on that date and at that hour.

(Signed)   MARSHAL FOCH.

The acceptance by Germany of the Allies' terms (the full text of which will be found below) means the end of the war, as the safeguards included will make it impossible for Germany to renew the struggle.

headlines: 'Germany's humiliation' – 'How the mighty are fallen' – 'End of the Great War' – 'Last shot fired'. But triumphalism was tempered by a respectful solemnity, acknowledging the high price paid by those who would not be returning. The *Western Gazette* wrote simply:

> 'An armistice with Germany was concluded on Monday – our 1,561st day of war. The conditions were signed at five o'clock in the morning, after a discussion which lasted all night. They took effect six hours later. At 11 o'clock in the forenoon the last shot of the great war was fired.'

Crowds took to the streets in spontaneous celebration and all over South Dorset, flags were hung from windows, church bells rang, streamers were stretched from house to house, ships fired their guns and sounded their sirens, thanksgiving services were held, and most people took the day off work.

Late in the afternoon, agricultural labourer Robert Morley was discovered 'absolutely helpless with intoxication', slumped over the tank of his traction engine, which had come to rest on an embankment between Littlemayne and Loscombe Wood, south of Dorchester. Morley explained to magistrates that he had been celebrating but, as he had not eaten anything, the beer 'got the best of him'. The court imposed a fine of £1, reminding him of the danger to which he had exposed the public.

The holiday mood continued for many weeks. Hundreds of American sailors came ashore from ships anchored in Portland Roads, and they mixed affably with returning British Tommies and Australian soldiers who were waiting to go home. Dances and games were held most afternoons and evenings by the American YMCA, which locals were welcome to attend, and the Jubilee Hall in Weymouth staged a show that, according to the local press, went down a storm with the Americans:

> 'An excellent bill of fare was made up for the amusement of the visitors, consisting of vaudeville turns and a most entertaining series of pictures. The remarkable film depicting the surrender of the German fleet, it is needless to say, was met with rapturous and mirthful shouts of approbation. Portraits of the King and other prominent personalities, both naval and military, who have overthrown the Hun, were also received with remarkable displays of patriotic enthusiasm.'

Generosity was in the air and the Board of Guardians at Weymouth Workhouse decided to give inmates extra fare that Christmas, along with the usual supply of beer – 'if procurable'. The town's schoolchildren were out of luck, however, when the School Attendance Committee met. Owing to the influenza epidemic, many schools had been forced to close that winter and in consequence 'children had been running wild for some eight or nine weeks'. It was therefore decided that the Christmas holidays should be restricted to just ten days, with pupils returning to their lessons on 30 December.

There was also disappointment for the people of Portland, who had organised a grand procession in December from Castletown to Easton Square. Sadly, the star of the event – a tank – failed to turn up on time, leaving airmen, soldiers, prison officers, boy scouts and girl guides to proceed without it.

And so began the return of servicemen to home shores. First were men with jobs to come back to or those whose skills were in demand. The rest had to wait their turn, remaining at the Front to perform duties such as battlefield clearance. There simply wasn't enough employment for everyone to return at once and Britain's demobilisation process would not finish until 1922.

When the celebrations had died down, reminders of the conflict were never far away for those who cared to look. William Swailes of Portland attended school in Greenwich and on returning at the end of each term he recalled:

'My mother would come to Weymouth Station to meet me ... On the station there was also another lady waiting. We saw her often waiting, but she never met anyone. We enquired about her and found that her son had gone away to volunteer for the army and had left by the train. He was killed, but for years she used to go to the station. Terrible thing.'

For others there were happy reunions. Private B. Higgins, who had lived with his mother in Weymouth, joined the army in 1916 and served on the Western Front. When he disappeared during the German offensive in March 1918 he was posted missing, presumed killed. In fact, he had been wounded and taken prisoner. Without any proper medical treatment he was set to work on the German railways, then in East Prussia tree felling. He would later describe conditions as shocking, and recalled the plight of another prisoner from Weymouth who was held in a cage at a cotton factory with around 8,000 other PoWs. When the Armistice was signed Higgins was released and arrived home in early December 'to the great joy of his mother and friends'. Yet, due to the effects of gas for which he had never been treated, Higgins had difficulty in speaking.

Many of those who made it home found it hard to come to terms with the horrors they had experienced. One such former soldier turned into a recluse in the village of Portesham, cruelly taunted as 'gun-shy Jack' by children who knew no better. Others were diagnosed with shell shock and underwent new methods of treatment like psychotherapy and hypnotherapy, with varying results. The majority of men shut the war away and looked forward as best they could.

Grief lurked behind the doors and shutters of homes, rich and poor. The wealthy Pope family of Dorchester had lost three of their ten sons, all of whom saw active service. (An eleventh son had died of tuberculosis in 1901.) Their father, Alfred, was a well-established businessman in the town, a partner in the brewery Eldridge Pope and Co, a former mayor, and a friend of Thomas Hardy. His family had two fine homes, one at South Court, South Walks Road in Dorchester, and another at Wrackleford, Stratton.

The first Pope to die was the fifth son, Percy, a 33-year-old lawyer who was on holiday in Paris when war was declared. His immediate thought was to seek out the Foreign Legion but he returned home to join the Welsh Regiment and was commissioned as a second lieutenant. He departed for the Western Front in 1915 and was killed in action that October, during an assault on German trenches near Loos, which involved hand-to-hand fighting. His body was never found and his family had to wait until August 1916 before a letter arrived informing them that 'The Army Council are regretfully constrained to conclude that 2 Lt Pope is dead.'

Captain Charles Pope, 39, the third son, was working as a GP in Sussex when war broke out. He served with the Royal Army Medical Corps and met his end in May 1917 aboard a troopship, the *Transylvania*, when it was hit by a German torpedo and sank in the Mediterranean.

The eldest son, Lieutenant Colonel Edward Pope, 43, (known in the family as Alec) had followed his father into the brewing business. He served in France with the South Wales Borderers but returned home wounded in April 1917 and was thereafter deployed for home service only.

Captain Charles Pope was one of the three brothers in his family to die as a result of the war.
(Courtesy of John Broom).

A postcard sent from Turkish prison camp by Captain Sandes to his mother in Weymouth, August 1916 (it was re-directed to the address where she was staying). *(Courtesy of the Sandes family).*

Tragically, the war caught up with him in April 1919, when he was taken ill and died of 'disease contracted on active service'.

Tucked away among the working class homes of Dorchester, widow Edith Payne wept for her son David, 29, who had met the cruellest of ends thousands of miles away in Mesopotamia. A private in the 2nd Dorsets, he was one of 350 from the battalion who had survived the siege of Kut-al-Amara, only to be marched hundreds of miles across the baking desert to prison camps in Anatolia. Mrs Payne, who lived in Friary Lane, would have known little about the torture inflicted upon her son by his Turkish captors. Men already semi-starved and ill were forced to march with heavy loads, had their boots taken from them, were flogged and beaten, and received barely enough food. Some of those who could go no further were buried alive.

It is estimated that only 140 Dorsets were still living by the end of June 1916, among them Private Payne. He managed to reach the prison camp but, weakened by sand-fly fever, jaundice and malaria, he died in September 1916. A similar fate befell Private William Mahar, 27, whose family lived in Miller's Close near the River Frome, on the edge of Dorchester.

More fortunate was Captain Warren Sandes of Weymouth, who served with the Royal Engineers. He was also taken prisoner after the siege of Kut (see Chapter Three) but survived the desert march and the following two years in prison camp, probably helped by the fact that the Turks generally treated officers with more respect than lower ranks. Life as a prisoner of war was still harsh and Sandes and his fellow officers endured freezing winters, poor food, very little exercise, and isolation so stultifying that some feared they were losing their minds. 'We asked a recently arrived prisoner if he thought we were mad,' wrote Sandes to his mother in Weymouth. 'He replied that he had not noticed it, but thought we were "bored to tears", and he is right. There is

Photographs taken by Captain Warren Sandes, showing life in Turkish prison camp: a sentry is snapped during an unguarded moment, and captured British officers dress to keep warm during the freezing Anatolian winter.
(Courtesy of the Sandes family).

The wedding of Captain Warren Sandes and Sylvia Sneyd-Kynnersley in 1919. Also pictured are Sylvia's sisters: Madge (far left), Rosie (sitting, left) Kitty (sitting, second right) and their mother Margaret (sitting next to the bride). *(Courtesy of the Sandes family).*

nothing to say at meals so generally we say nothing.'

Never without his camera, Warren Sandes recorded prison life on film (often secretly). He also kept diaries and unsent letters from Kut in the hidden compartment of a wooden box, which he brought back to England when he was repatriated in November 1918. He used the diaries to write a book called *In Kut and Captivity*, published the following year.

In 1919 Captain Sandes married Sylvia Sneyd-Kynnersley – one of the four diary-writing sisters – and the couple had two children. In later years he was promoted to the rank of lieutenant colonel and became a well-respected military historian. Sandes rarely spoke about his experiences in Mesopotamia, but the memories of near-starvation in Kut never left him. 'Right to the end of his life, he had to know there was bread in the house, and he always had to have a piece of bread on the side of his plate, even though he never ate it,' recalled his daughter Penelope.

By the end of the war, some 120,000 Anzac soldiers had passed through Weymouth's convalescent camps (see Chapter Two). Some stayed just a week or two before returning to the Front, others spent months recuperating, and the more seriously wounded were shipped home. Time spent convalescing was rarely wasted. Training schools had been set up by the YMCA, intended to prepare men for the new world they would face when they returned home at the end of the conflict and equip them with skills to help them find work. Particularly popular was a course in motor mechanics and the internal combustion engine – new technology that was changing the face of agriculture and industry. In September 1918, around 20 qualified drivers and mechanics had been turned out, 35 were attending classes, and 75 were waiting to join. The YMCA had also secured 14 acres of land locally, where the latest methods in agriculture were being demonstrated, including irrigation, which many servicemen had seen used with great success in Egypt.

The Aussies had made themselves at home during their time in Weymouth. Local people welcomed them into their homes and treated them with warmth and generosity. Some soldiers tracked down members of their extended family who were still in England, surprising them on their doorsteps. Others struck up relationships with local girls whom they would marry and take home after the war. A few left behind babies who would grow up without fathers.

Local business boomed as a result of the Australian soldiers' additional custom and there were always plenty of adverts in *The Australian at Weymouth*, a newspaper produced for servicemen in the town. S. T. Abrahams, conveniently located opposite the Black Dog pub in St Mary Street, was proud to call himself 'The Aussies' photographer'. The Gloucester Street Sailors' and Soldiers' Club, just off the Esplanade, enjoyed using Australian bar-room

Local traders were sad to see the Aussies go, as these adverts suggest in the November 1918 edition of *The Australian at Weymouth*, a newspaper produced for the servicemen in the town. Chemists Stedman & Co thanked their Australian friends 'for the generous support they have given them during the past years'.
(Courtesy of Weymouth Museum).

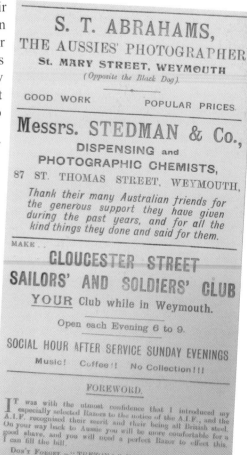

S. T. ABRAHAMS,
THE AUSSIES' PHOTOGRAPHER
St. MARY STREET, WEYMOUTH
(*Opposite the Black Dog*).

GOOD WORK   POPULAR PRICES.

Messrs. STEDMAN & Co.,
DISPENSING and
PHOTOGRAPHIC CHEMISTS,
87 ST. THOMAS STREET, WEYMOUTH.

Thank their many Australian friends for the generous support they have given during the past years, and for all the kind things they done and said for them.

MAKE ..

GLOUCESTER STREET
SAILORS' AND SOLDIERS' CLUB
YOUR Club while in Weymouth.

Open each Evening 6 to 9.

SOCIAL HOUR AFTER SERVICE SUNDAY EVENINGS
Music!   Coffee!!   No Collection!!!

FOREWORD.

IT was with the utmost confidence that I introduced my especially selected Razors to the notice of the A.I.F., and the A.I.F. recognised their merit and their being all British steel. On your way back to Aussie you will be more comfortable for a good shave, and you will need a perfect Razor to effect this. I can fill the bill.

Don't Forget.—"TREZONA" HAIR CREAM is non-greasy and fixes the most troublesome locks.

R. TREE, First-class Hairdresser,
89 ABBOTSBURY ROAD (Main Road to Camp),
WESTHAM (150 yards from Westham Camp).

Australian soldiers marching over the Town Bridge, Weymouth, on their way home in 1918.
(Courtesy of Weymouth Museum, Ref: LH/IL/PH/EV/019).

humour to advertise its social hour after church on Sunday: 'Music! Coffee!! No collection!!!'

When the war ended there was genuine sadness among some local traders, and the chemists Stedman & Co included this touching farewell in one of its adverts: 'Messrs Stedman & Co ... Thank their many Australian friends for the generous support they have given them during the past years, and for all the kind things they done [sic] and said for them.'

As troops began to depart, the barber R. Tree, whose premises were on Abbotsbury Road, made a last-ditch attempt to rake in some business: 'On your way back to Aussie you will be more comfortable for a good shave, and you will need a perfect razor to effect this. I can fit the bill,' read his advert, which finished with one final tip: 'Don't forget. "Trezona" hair cream is non-greasy and fixes the most troublesome locks.'

Today there are plenty of reminders of the Australians' sojourn in South Dorset. Queensland Road, Melbourne Street, Adelaide Crescent, Sydney Street and Perth Street can all be found in the Westham area of Weymouth, where the council bought up the Anzac camp and used it for housing after the war. In Chickerell, Australia Road can be found off Chickerell Road and it is a reminder of the nearby Monte Video camp, and an Australian flag presented to the village by departing troops still hangs in St Mary's Church. In local cemeteries there are gravestones of soldiers who died at camp in Weymouth and an Anzac memorial, cut from bright Portland stone, stands on the town seafront with the inscription 'They came from afar in the cause of freedom.'

During the war years, the people of Dorchester grew accustomed to their German 'visitors' at the prison camp situated to the west of the town. PoWs were often seen out and about sweeping streets, working in parks and gardens, labouring on local farms, or being hired out to help in local businesses. The novelist Thomas Hardy recruited one PoW to work in the garden of his Dorchester home, Max Gate.

The Germans aroused interest among townspeople who were curious to see what 'the enemy' looked like up close, and in general they were treated well and with respect. Military funerals were accorded any prisoner who died in camp. A gun carriage would take the coffin to Fordington Cemetery in processions that were held during the early morning, before the traffic built up, and often drew large crowds.

Details were reported in local newspapers, for instance in June 1916 the *Western Gazette* described how the coffin of one prisoner, who had

Departing German prisoners on their final march through Dorchester in 1919. *(Courtesy of Dr Colin Chapman).*

died of appendicitis, was escorted (under armed guard) by 120 prisoners 'looking well in their blue-grey uniforms and top boots, and marching with martial stride'. At the burial service, a hymn was sung by a party of prisoners: 'In the quietude of the morning the unaccompanied singing, resonant and harmonious, was very effective.' They then filed past the grave, each dropping a handful of earth on to the coffin.

The repatriation of the German prisoners did not begin until the spring of 1919 when, just as quickly as they had first appeared during the summer of 1914, the PoWs departed. Parties were marched through the town to Dorchester West Station, where they boarded trains, probably for Plymouth or Bristol. They were then shipped back to a country that was hardly recognizable, reeling in defeat and with a population half-starved as a result of the Allied blockade of German ports.

It is estimated that between 8,000 and 10,000 German prisoners passed through Dorchester between 1914 and 1919. During the decades that followed the camp was largely forgotten by the town, although interest has been renewed by the First World War Centenary. Also forgotten was the

The German memorial at Fordington Cemetery to prisoners who died at Dorchester Prison Camp. *(Photographs by the author).*

German memorial at Fordington Cemetery commemorating the 45 PoWs who died at the camp and were buried in the churchyard. Designed and carved by prisoners themselves, it bears the inscription: *'Hier ruhen Deutsche Krieger in fremder Erde doch unvergessen'* ('Here lie German soldiers in a foreign land but not forgotten').

Among the names is Frank Radgowski, a 20-year-old Polish soldier who tried to escape early one morning in May 1919. He was shot by sentries who found him with wire cutters, on the barbed wire perimeter fence. Asked why he had tried to escape, Radgowski replied, just before he died: 'I wanted to go home.'

In 1963 the prisoners buried at Fordington were exhumed and reburied at Cannock Chase German Military Cemetery, Staffordshire, along with some 2,000 fellow PoWs from around Britain, but the memorial remains.

It is testament to the decent conditions in which prisoners were held that only 45 died. International agreements about the treatment of PoWs already existed in 1914, and Dorchester underwent regular inspections throughout the war by observers from neutral countries. It is interesting to note that the photo on page 38, showing the Dorchester camp's wooden huts, was one of a series taken by the International Committee of the Red Cross, during an inspection.

Most of Dorchester's prison camp deaths came late in the war, between 1918 and 1919, and were caused by the deadly infection known as Spanish flu that would eventually kill more worldwide (estimates range from 50 to 100 million) than had perished in the conflict. Nobody knows for sure where the virus originated, but symptoms were first noticed in the rancid trenches of France in spring 1918. As the British servicemen returned home, so it travelled with them and the first cases in Britain appeared in Glasgow, during May 1918. The illness crept up stealthily, affecting the young as well as the old, and people couldn't always be sure that danger was imminent until it was upon them. The first signs were a runny nose, coughing and sneezing, then muscles and joints began to ache, with fever and severe fatigue following. Although many recovered, some went on to develop pneumonia which could prove fatal.

In October 1918, at home in Greenhill Terrace, Weymouth, Margaret Sneyd-Kynnersley was recording in her diary all the splendid news from Europe, whilst also keeping one eye on the Spanish flu. There seemed no reason to worry until the end of the month, when her youngest daughter, Rosie, who worked as a Red Cross nurse, became unwell:

19 October – 'Ostend, Lille & Rouen taken – glorious news – lovely.'

23 October – 'Terrible epidemic of Spanish influenza.'

24 October – 'Sylvia & I gardened and cleaned, great offensive on the Scheldt.'

27 October (Sunday) – 'Influenza so bad none of us went to church. Loveliest day, sat in garden in morning.'

29 October – 'Influenza really bad. Austria asks for a separate peace.'

30 October – 'Rosie in bed with a cold, eating well.'

31 October – 'Darling Rosie has influenza I fear. Dr Wetherall came in evening – bed, warmth and hot drinks.'

During the next few weeks Rosie became progressively worse and her mother's diary entries were sporadic. On 2 November: 'Dr Wetherall came, all of us anxious about darling Rosie, she seems to be going on well, much perspiration. Made quince marmalade and tomato sauce.' Two days later came a hammer blow: 'Rosie – double pneumonia.' As Rosie fought for her life, Mrs Sneyd-Kynnersley could only face writing a few words on 11 November, Armistice Day: 'End of the war. Too anxious about Rosie to think of anything else but thank God for the terrible war ending.'

It wasn't until the beginning of December that the crisis was over and Rosie slowly began to recover. Her mother sighed with relief: 'Once again I can write in this book. Such a terrible time it has been since I last wrote. Thank God over and over again my darling Rosie is spared to us. Dr Wetherall came and said she is well but care needed to prevent her heart being dilated. A very wet day.'

Rosie made a full recovery, but Spanish flu claimed the lives of some 228,000 civilians in Britain, including many in Dorset.

***

Peace was not formally agreed until the signing of the Treaty of Versailles in June 1919, but the Armistice was a signal for most people to put the conflict behind them and start to rebuilding their lives. Nevertheless, the fighting wasn't over everywhere, as conflicts spawned by the Great War were still ongoing in other parts of the world. War continued in Western and Northern Russia between the communist Bolsheviks, who had overthrown the Tsar in 1917, and the Royalist White Russians. The latter were supported by Allied troops of all nations – British, American, French, Italian, Slavs – and in May 1919 volunteers from the Dorchester Regiment joined a composite British battalion, which sailed to the far north of Russia to join them (with a promise of two months' leave at the end).

Also on his way northwards was a young Weymouth naval officer, 18-year-old Sub Lieutenant Archie Dunn. After finishing work sweeping for mines off the coast of Ireland, he had just been appointed First Lieutenant of the minesweeper HMS *Sword Dance* and, although normally a man who showed little emotion, he couldn't hide his delight:

Archie Dunn with his girlfriend, Bobbie, in Weymouth before departing for Northern Russia; and with men from the Naval Brigade, cooking over a camp fire on the bank of the River Dvina. (Below) The *Sword Dance* sinks after hitting a mine. *(Courtesy of the Dunn family).*

'*Sword Dance*: twin screw tunnel minesweeper 1-6 pdr, 6 Lewis guns, 12 mines. 10kts, oil fuel. 130x26x5. Some ship!' he wrote in his diary.

The *Sword Dance* was part of a Royal Naval flotilla tasked with supporting the White Russians. It would play a vital role on the Dvina River, in clearing the way for Allied forces to bombard Bolsheviks hiding out in dense riverbank forests.

Before departure, Dunn spent a few days at home in Weymouth finding a good home for his beloved motorbike, meeting up with friends for a round of golf at Came, and saying goodbye to his mother and his

girlfriend, Bobbie (who would later become his wife). But he was impatient to leave. On his final day, 27 April 1919, he noted in his diary: 'Church. Went down to Weymouth,' then added with ironic melodrama, 'Tea and good bye for ever with B [Bobbie]. Mo bought my bike for £20. Mother and B don't want me to go.'

In Russia, lawlessness hung in the air with rumours of mutiny among Russian and Allied troops as well as looting, and reports of executions. ('A woman spy was shot last night; had to dig her own grave,' wrote Dunn.) In the sweltering summer heat, work was dangerous and often carried out under heavy shellfire, and the fighting was as fierce as anything on the Western Front.

In June the *Sword Dance* struck a mine and sank. 'Worked on saving gear till 3am. Some deserted the ship,' wrote Dunn, who was later awarded the DSC for his attempts to save the vessel. He and the men of the Dorsets finally returned home in autumn 1919.

***

The war left scars on country villages as well as the towns and cities of Britain, and when men didn't return from the fighting their loss was keenly felt by small communities where everybody knew each other. To the west of Weymouth, Abbotsbury lost 13 of its men and at Portesham 14 never returned. Yet, in neighbouring Langton Herring, overlooking the Fleet Water, 31 men (around one fifth of its population) saw active service – and all came home. Their names can be seen on a roll of honour at the village's tiny St Peter's Church.

The 1911 Census shows that at the turn of the century, Langton Herring had a lot of single men working as tradesmen or on farms who still lived at home with their parents. For them the chance to go and fight must have sounded like an adventure too good to miss. It would have been a welcome break in the routine lives of men like Stanley Wederell, who was in his early twenties when war broke out, an apprentice wheelwright living at 'School House' with his father, a gardener, his mother, a schoolmistress, and two younger sisters. Or Albert Taylor, then in his mid-thirties, who worked as a bricklayer and shared a home with his widowed mother and younger brother. Their details are recorded in the 1911 Census, and it is likely that their names correspond to those on the roll of honour: S. Wederell of the Dorset Regiment, A. J. Taylor of the Royal Naval Reserve.

Also on the roll of honour were men higher up Langton Herring's

C.F. BAILEY	R. SUSSEX
C.E. CASE	WILTS
T. CARTER	R.N.
J.P. FARQUHARSON	COMM. R.N. OBE D.S.O.
F.A. FARQUHARSON	K.G.O. SAPPER M.C.
K.R. FARQUHARSON	L⸺ COMM. R.N. D.S.C.
E.R. FARQUHARSON	L⸺ R.N.
C. FERNS	C.G.
E.W. GARRETT	L. CORPS
H.M. GREENHILL	MAJOR DORSETS
F.J. HANSFORD	R.G.A.
A. HARRIS	R.N.
A.J. THATCHER	R.F.A.
W. LARCOMBE	R. INNISKILLINGS
F. MATHEWS	C.G.
E. MOWLAM	L. CORPS
G. MOWLAM	R.N.
J. MOWLAM	R.N.
S.C. MOWLAM	M.G.C.
W.E. MOWLAM	WORCESTERS
H.J. PENFOLD	C.G
S. PEACH	WILTS
R. RANDALL	R.G.A.
E.A. SPARKS	R.A.S.C. M.T.
B.O. SMYTHE	CAPT. NORTHANTS OBE
C. STONE	R.N.
C. STONE	R.N.
W. STONE	R.N.
A.J. TAYLOR	R.N.R.
S. WEDERELL	DORSET
W.J. WHITTLE	R.A.V.C.

The roll of honour at St Peter's Church listing all the men who returned to Langton Herring. *(Photograph by the author).*

social ladder. E. A. Sparks of the Royal Army Service Corps was probably Edward Sparks, the local squire and a man of private means, who lived at the Rectory. The four Farquharsons were the sons of Archibald Farquharson, a retired naval commander who lived at the Manor House.

Today Langton Herring is known as a 'thankful village', to which all the men returned safely from the First World War – the only one in Dorset and one of just 53 throughout Britain. It is also known as a 'doubly thankful village', because all of its servicemen would survive the Second World War too... But that is another story.

Peace and tranquillity at St Peter's Church, Langton Herring, the only 'thankful village' in Dorset (of 53 across Britain), to which all those who served in the Great War returned. *(Photograph by the author).*

Bibliography

Barrett Duncan, *Men of Letters, the Post Office Heroes who Fought the Great War* (AA Publishing, 2014).

Bates Brian, *Dorchester Remembers the Great War* (Roving Press, 2012).

Carter Geoffrey, *The Royal Navy at Portland Since 1845* (Maritime Books, 1987).

Clammer Richard, *Cosens of Weymouth 1848-1918 – A History of the Bournemouth, Weymouth and Swanage Paddle Steamers* (Black Dwarf Publications, 2005).

Doyle Peter, *First World War Britain* (Shire Publications, 2012).

Gosling Lucinda (in association with Mary Evans Picture Library), *Knitting for Tommy – Keeping the Great War Soldier Warm* (The History Press, 2014).

Graves Robert, *Goodbye to All That (*Penguin Modern Classics, 1960).
Jarvis Major C.S. , *Happy Yesterdays* (Country Life, 1948).

Legg Rodney, *Dorset in the First World War* (Dorset Books, 2012).

Mark Graham, *Prisoners of War in British Hands During WW1 – A Study of Their History, the Camps and Their Mails* (The Postal History Society, 2007).

McCosker Anne, *Lieutenant Martin's Letters: FWS Martin, MM, an Anzac in the Great War* (Reveille Press, 2013).

Morris Stuart, *Portland: An Illustrated History* (Dovecote Press, 1985).

Sandes Major E.W.C., *In Kut and Captivity with the Sixth Indian Division,* (John Murray, 1919).

West Nigel, *Historical Dictionary of World War I Intelligence* (Scarecrow Press, 2013).

Other Sources

CONTEMPORARY REPORTS FROM local newspapers are used throughout the book and these were read on microfilm at Weymouth Library and Dorset History Centre, and online at the British Newspaper Archive (**http://britishnewspaperarchive.co.uk**). Also scattered throughout the book are the colourful memories of children who grew up on Portland during the Great War; these are preserved by the Portland Heritage Trust and most were originally recorded as oral histories.

Privately-held collections of diaries, photographs and other memorabilia were generously shared by the following: the Dunn family (Archibald Dunn's war in northern Russia); Tina Morley (Maggie Watson's autograph book); the

Sandes family (the Sneyd-Kynnersley diaries and Warren Sandes' experiences in Kut and captivity); Richard Samways (memories of Edward Samways and Ernest Patterson); and Eric Scott (the internment of Heinrich Schutte).

Other sources are listed below. Picture credits are given in the captions and all reasonable efforts have been made to identify the owners of images used in this book.

CHAPTER 1

Major C. S. Jarvis and the German spy – an extract from the Major's memoir *Happy Yesterdays* (see Bibliography) can be found at Weymouth Library (Ref: L.940.4 JA.1).

Sergeant Major George Beck and the Christmas Truce – George Beck's Great War diaries are held by Dorset History Centre (Ref: D.1820/1/7).

Winston Churchill's description of the Grand Fleet's departure from Portland Harbour in 1914 can be found at **http://www.winstonchurchill.org**.

CHAPTER 2

Dorchester Prison Camp – I am indebted to Dr Colin R. Chapman, a leading authority on WW1 prison camps in Britain, for generously sharing his research and images. For those interested in further reading, Dr Chapman has co-written a book on the subject: *Detained in England: 1914-20 Eastcote PoW Camp Pattishall* (Lochin Publishing, 2012).

Employment of German prisoners at Upwey House – the letter to Mr B. Butler Bowden from Dorchester Prison Camp can be found at Weymouth Library, Ref: LB/Bow BO.1.

The Nursing Times – extracts relating to Weymouth in the Great War are held by Weymouth Library (Ref: L.940.476 Nu.1).

Reports of the tragic incident concerning Private James Gribbin can be found in the 1915 *British Journal of Nursing* at **http://rcnarchive.rcn.org.uk**.

Maggie Watson's autograph book is reproduced on the Western Front Association's website **http://westernfrontassociation.com** (click 'People' – 'Reflections' – 'Montevideo Camp').

The Anzacs in Weymouth – particularly useful were articles by George Lanning in the *Dorset Year Books* of 1990 & 1992 (published by the Society of Dorset Men), which are held at Weymouth Library; also '*Chickerell 'Yer Tiz'* – *An illustrated Compilation of Historical and Social Information'*, published by Chickerell Parish Council, 1997.

The story of Fred Martin is told in full by Anne McCosker in her book *Lieutenant Martin's Letters* (see Bibliography).

The letters of Bert Smythe can be found at **http://smythe.id.au/index.htm**.

CHAPTER 3

The Portland School logs are preserved by the Portland Heritage Trust. The letter from S. James to the Otter family of Portland in 1915 is held by Weymouth Museum (Ref: LH/WA/092).

CHAPTER 4

The story of Dorset's 'secret tanks' is told on the BBC's 'World War One At Home' pages at **http://www.bbc.co.uk/ww1**.

The annual reports of Cosens & Co during the Great War can be found at Weymouth Library (Ref L.387.5.cos.1).

The wartime records of the Easton Ladies Sewing Guild and Easton Ladies Working Guild are held at Portland Heritage Trust.

Records of the criminal trials at Dorchester Assizes during the Great War can be found at Dorset History Centre.

CHAPTER 5

The story of the Pope family of Dorchester is told by Brian Bates in his book *Dorchester Remembers the Great War* (see Bibliography) and by John Broom in posts at **http://www.faithinworldwartwo.blogspot.co.uk**.

Author Biography

JACQUELINE WADSWORTH is a freelance writer and lives near Bristol with her family. She has written two other books to coincide with the WW1 Centenary: *Letters from the Trenches* and *Bristol in the Great War,* both published by Pen & Sword Books. When not at her desk she is a keen cyclist, follower of Liverpool FC, fan of American roots music, and supporter of The Donkey Sanctuary. You can read her blog at **http://www.soldierletters. blogspot.co.uk** and follow her on Twitter: **@soldiersletters**.

The author Jacqueline Wadsworth.

Index